*Elizabet*

The whole world was shocked at photos of Elizabeth Taylor—grossly overweight, her beauty gone, her health ruined by alcohol and painkillers. Then suddenly there was Liz on the cover of America's magazines—gorgeously slim and sexy, fantastically beautiful, radiantly happy. Now we all can find out the truth about the tragedies that nearly destroyed her—and how Elizabeth Taylor fought back for a new image, new self-respect, and new happiness as an independent woman at last!

- Her health problems . . . and her heartbreaks
- Coping with back pain . . . a legacy from *National Velvet*
- Liz and her children . . . how they helped her recover
- Robert Wagner . . . the friendship that lasted through tragedy
- Helping other alcoholics—including close friend Liza Minnelli—with her courage
- The fat lady within . . . keeping those pounds off forever
- Liz and all those fabulous rings . . . what really happened with John Warner, Victor Luna, and Dennis Stein.

*Plus facts about her beauty and diet regimes . . . a revealing look at the beautiful new Elizabeth!*

# The New Elizabeth

## Marianne Robin-Tani

ST. MARTIN'S PRESS/NEW YORK

THE NEW ELIZABETH: BETTER AND MORE BEAUTIFUL THAN EVER

Copyright © 1988 by Marianne Robin-Tani

Library of Congress Catalog Card Number: 87-62617

ISBN: 0-312-90949-7    Can. ISBN: 0-312-90950-0

Printed in the United States of America

First St. Martin's Press mass market edition/February 1988

10  9  8  7  6  5  4  3  2  1

**To my mom and dad**
*who were always there for love, support,
encouragement, and midnight spelling checks*

The author would like to sincerely thank the following for their infinite assistance and forbearance:

The Academy of Motion Picture Arts &
    Sciences Library
Yoko Asano
Hether Churchill
El Camino College Library
Janna Wong-Healy
Jenny Huerta
Mona Kim
Los Angeles County Public Library System
Skip E. Lowe
Anne Lowenkopf
Ann and Jack Lowenkopf
Sheldon Lowenkopf
Madeleine Morel
Kathleen Robin-Lowry and Scott Lowry
Sam Rubin
Kaz and Jenny Sakamoto
Susan Shimotsuka
Cynthia Takano
Noriyasu Tani
Richard Taylor
UCLA Theater Arts Library
Hiro "Ushi-chan" Ushijima
Dennis Umeda
Ethlie Ann Vare
Cathleen Young.

The material in this book was gathered from personal interviews and from information gleaned from the following sources:

*A Valuable Property, the Life Story of Michael Todd,* Michael Todd, Jr. and Susan McCarthy Todd
*American Film*
*The Barbara Walters Special*
*Boxoffice*
*Burton,* Hollis Alpert
*California Living*
*Chicago Tribune*
*Cosmopolitan*
*Current Biography Yearbook, 1985*
*Daily News*
*Drama-logue*
*Elizabeth, the Life and Career of Elizabeth Taylor,* Dick Sheppard
*Elizabeth Taylor,* Elizabeth Taylor
*Elizabeth Taylor, the Last Star,* Kitty Kelley
*50 Plus*
*Film Comment*
*Globe*
*Good Housekeeping*
*Good Morning America*
*Harper's Bazaar*
*Hollywood Reporter*
*Idol, Rock Hudson,* Jerry Oppenheimer and Jack Vitek
*Interview*

*Jet*
*Ladies' Home Journal*
*Life*
*Look*
*Los Angeles*
Los Angeles *Herald-Examiner*
*Los Angeles Times*
*Los Angeles Times Magazine*
*McCall's*
*Montgomery Clift, a Biography,* Patricia Bosworth
*My Life! My Loves!,* Eddie Fisher
*National Enquirer*
*The New Republic*
*Newsweek*
*New York*
*New York Times*
*The Nine Lives of Michael Todd,* Art Cohn
*People*
*Photoplay*
*Richard Burton, Very Close Up,* John Cottrell and
     Fergus Cashin
*Saturday Evening Post*
*Screen International*
*Time*
*TV Guide*
*Us*
*USA Today*
*Vanity Fair*
*Variety*
*Vogue*
Washington *Post*
*Who's Afraid of Elizabeth Taylor?,* Brenda
     Maddox
*Woman's World*
*Working Woman.*

# Prologue

SHE is indisputably one of the most gorgeous creatures ever born on this planet. Her acting abilities have been toasted with the finest champagne everywhere from tiny hamlets in the middle of nowhere to the most luxurious spots on earth. Everything about her personal life has been found newsworthy—her romances and tragedies are particularly fascinating—but the woman can make headlines by buying a new bauble or even sneezing.

Yet, despite the glamorous life-style, the global adulation, and the untold riches, Elizabeth Taylor was never truly happy.

She hid behind the veil of her talents and her incredible beauty. She flaunted her men and her jewels, trying to ward off the grim specter that was gnawing at her insides.

But little by little, the dark demon deep inside her was winning. Over the years she turned from a sweet, obedient child into a willful, obscenity-spouting virago. Insecurities caused her to jump in and out of

1

marriages and engagements faster than most people change their hairstyles. Her voracious appetites for food and alcohol blew her up into nearly unrecognizable obesity, which caused the world to turn away with a wince. And her constant health problems sent her into a nightmare spiral of drug dependence which lasted half her life.

By all accounts—her own included—fifty-one-year-old Elizabeth should have been dead by the end of 1983. Although none of the various illnesses, accidents, and stressful periods she'd endured had managed to do her in, her heavy drinking and addiction to pain-killers were coming dangerously close to pushing her over the edge.

While fate has willed that her life be filled with harrowing tragedies, she seems destined for a happy ending. Unlike contemporaries such as Judy Garland and Marilyn Monroe, who succumbed under fame's glare to their own misery and excesses, Elizabeth stopped herself just in time. Her admittance into the Betty Ford Center on December 5, 1983, undoubtedly saved her life.

Seven weeks later, when she walked out the clinic's doors back into the real world, Elizabeth was filled with startling new emotions. She was definitely stronger and healthier than she had been in years. In addition, she had discovered that she was a good person, worthy of her own respect.

During the next few years Elizabeth would slowly build on these new emotions; her pride in herself would enable her self-confidence to continue to grow. As she began to take her life into her own hands, molding herself into what *she* wanted to be, she also began to feel a rare tranquility.

For the first time in her life, Elizabeth Taylor could honestly love herself. Finally, this most beautiful and gifted of women has found true happiness.

# Chapter One

*"My toughest role is trying to grow up."*
—Elizabeth Taylor

EVERYONE felt sorry for Francis and Sara Taylor. Howard, their golden-haired first child, was so beautiful that he was often glowingly compared to the angel children in Botticelli paintings.

But about this new baby girl, my God, it was hard to be polite. The child was so ugly, it was difficult to believe that she was even born to the same set of parents. Thick dark hair covered her body; her skin was a molted, blotchy red; and her eyes were screwed tightly shut the first ten days after her birth. Even her mother recoiled when the infant was first placed in her arms.

Then the baby finally opened her eyes. They were magnificent, a haunting violet color. Although it took her a long time to learn how to walk and talk, Elizabeth Rosemond Taylor learned early on how to charm an audience and keep them captive in her alluring gaze.

Three years after her birth in London on February 27, 1932, little Elizabeth was already dancing with the other tots her age in a recital at the famed studio of

4

Madame Vacani. All the diminutive fairies, butterflies, and angels fluttered around the stage a few times, then properly withdrew.

All except one. When the curtain rose, a solitary child in her butterfly costume struck a pose in the center of the stage. Her raven-black hair hung in charming ringlets around her rosy cheeks and her amazing blue-violet eyes sparkled at the audience. Captivated by her dazzling smile, the audience began to applaud thunderously as the child charmingly circled the stage a couple more times before being snatched back into the wings.

"It was a marvelous feeling on that stage," Elizabeth remembers. "The isolation, the hugeness, the feeling of space and no end to space."

She knew immediately that this was where she belonged, and the center stage is where she has remained her entire life.

Elizabeth spent her first seven years growing up in an English fairy tale. As an art dealer in London, her father had made the acquaintance of many rich and powerful people. One such family, the Cazalets, shared the Taylors' Christian Science religion and loved little Elizabeth and Howard as their own.

Patriarch Victor Cazalet was called "Godfather" by Elizabeth, and provided the Taylors with a quaint fourteen-room sixteenth-century "cottage" named "Little Swallows" for their weekends and summer vacations. He also gave Elizabeth her first pony and saw to it that she learned how to ride.

The Taylors' life in London was very comfortable indeed, much more comfortable than either Sara or Francis had known growing up in quiet Arkansas City, a small Kansas town located on the Oklahoma border. In addition to Elizabeth's dancing lessons, she and Howard also attended exclusive private schools and were cared for by a nanny. Elizabeth was born in their city home, a lovely neo-Georgian house located at 8 Wildwood Road, overlooking Hampstead Heath.

Francis Taylor had been employed as an art dealer for his wealthy uncle, Howard Young, since he was sixteen. While working in Uncle Howard's New York gallery, he became reacquainted with his former school chum Sara Warmbrodt, a beauty who was happily making a name for herself as Sara Sothern by starring in the Edward Everett Horton repertory group's production of *The Fool*. After their marriage in 1926, Sara gave up the stage, and Uncle Howard quickly dispatched the handsome young couple across the Atlantic to be his European agents.

While residing in Britain, little Elizabeth suffered the first of her lifelong string of serious illnesses and unusual accidents. Less than a year old, she badly burned a finger when she touched a red-hot electric fire in the grate. In March, 1935, she developed a throat infection so severe that her abscessed ears had to be lanced twice daily for four days, and she was in bed for three weeks with a constant temperature of 103°. Her parents consented to call a doctor, but were sure that her recovery was a direct result of the power of their prayers. Elizabeth's first pony, Betty, threw her into a patch of stinging nettles right after the youngster got on her back for an introductory ride. A year later she fell into a creek and nearly drowned before Howard managed to rescue her.

By 1939 the threat of imminent war sent Sara and

her two children sailing on the last trip of the liner *Manhattan,* toward a new life in Pasadena, California, where Sara's grandfather owned a chicken ranch.

"Elizabeth had never seen a film before she came to America," Sara remembers. "She saw a Shirley Temple film coming over on the boat, and she thought it was so much fun."

The family's surroundings—and circumstances—were radically different in America. Gone were the manor house, summer home, chauffeur, and servants. Now enrolled in public school, Elizabeth's English accent was held up as a paragon of perfect speech, and her teachers invited her into a faculty meeting to tell them firsthand about the situation in England. Naturally, her boisterous classmates teased her mercilessly now that she was the new teacher's pet.

Francis arrived a few months later with crates of paintings and swept the family off to live in Pacific Palisades while he opened up an art gallery in the old Chateau Elysée in Hollywood. About a year later he moved the gallery to the Beverly Hills Hotel.

Prior to leaving London, Victor Cazalet wrote Francis a letter of introduction to his old friend, art lover Hedda Hopper. Hedda visited Francis' gallery, purchased a painting of gypsies' heads, then gave the Taylors their first plug in her column: "a new find—eight-year-old Elizabeth Taylor, whose mother was Sara Sothern, the lame girl in the play *The Fool,* and whose father, Francis Taylor, has just opened an exhibition of paintings by Augustus John in the Beverly Hills Hotel."

During the late 1930's child stars such as Shirley Temple and Deanna Durbin were all the rage in Hollywood (to say nothing of saving their respective studios from the brink of bankruptcy), and Hedda Hopper's item about "discovering" a gorgeous new child made the industry folks look twice at young Elizabeth.

Sara dragged her beautiful little girl everywhere she went, and over and over people said the same thing: "That child is the image of Vivien Leigh. Get her over to Selznick's. They're testing for the part of Scarlett O'Hara's daughter." Turning a deaf ear on Elizabeth's desperate pleas for such an action, Sara vetoed the idea. At the time, Francis applauded his wife's decision to keep their little girl's childhood a "normal" one.

But Hollywood being what it was, and Elizabeth's natural inclinations being what they were, it was impossible to keep the two separated for long. Her classmates in grade school were the children of Norma Shearer and Darryl F. Zanuck; she once had a crush on John Derek; and her singing teacher—Andre De Segurola—also taught Deanna Durbin.

Elizabeth was soon spotted by another art lover with connections in the film world: Andrea Cowdin, wife of Universal's chairman of the board, Cheever Cowdin. She recalls that Elizabeth was "the most beautiful child I have ever seen. She did not walk, she danced. She was so merry, so full of love for every living thing, whether it was a person, an animal, or a flower. She had a lovely singing voice, too."

Andrea immediately told Sara that "Cheever must see this child." When entertained by Sara and Elizabeth at tea, Cheever was duly impressed and told the mother to bring the daughter in for a screen test. Sara again demurred over Elizabeth's rising pleas.

A short time later, Elizabeth's impromptu singing of

"The Blue Danube" before her dancing lesson caught the attention of Carmen Considine, wife of Metro-Goldwyn-Mayer producer John W. Considine, Jr. She convinced her husband to set up an appointment to see Elizabeth, and after hearing the child sing a few scales, immediately dragged her down the hall to see the big boss—Louis B. Mayer.

Although he was just then rushing off to a meeting, Mayer eyed the girl and shouted, "Well, what are you waiting for? Sign her up! Sign her up!"

Elizabeth was in seventh heaven. MGM had offered her a contract at $100 per week, with yearly options, for seven years. She begged and pleaded with Sara to sign it. She promised her mother anything in the world.

But Sara decided to play a little politics. She next took Elizabeth over to Universal and coyly let it be known that MGM had a contract ready for her daughter. Without even giving her a screen test, Cowdin immediately doubled MGM's offer.

By this time Elizabeth knew that Universal wasn't the place for her. "Elizabeth loved it at MGM. She begged me to sign with them. She kept saying 'Mother, I *know* it's *right* for me to be *here*. . . . I *know* it's *right*,'" Sara says.

Universal was chosen because Sara felt that her daughter wouldn't get lost at the smaller studio. "We couldn't have been more mistaken in our decision!" she said later.

During her year at Universal, the girl was only given three days' work. She played a bratty little girl named Alpha Switzer in an hour-long film called *Man or Mouse*. A few years later it was reissued as *There's One*

*Born Every Minute,* but nothing had changed except the title.

One year and dozens of singing lessons later, casting director Dan Kelly was none too eager to re-sign the raven-haired darling. "The kid has nothing," he said. "Her eyes are too old. She doesn't have the face of a kid." Nine-year-old Elizabeth's contract was not renewed.

The grapevine let MGM know that she'd been dropped, and the huge studio in Culver City with "More Stars Than There Are in Heaven" offered her another chance. Again Sara says that Elizabeth "sang and danced and *begged* Daddy and me to *please, please* sign a contract with MGM." Her parents gave in and she joined the star factory to end all star factories.

By now the Taylors were living in a Mediterranean-style home with a red tile roof on tree-lined Elm Drive in Beverly Hills. Elizabeth's first role at the new studio came after Francis met producer Sam Marx at a meeting of the neighborhood's air-raid wardens. Francis had heard that Marx was looking for a little girl who spoke with an English accent to play the role of the duke's granddaughter in *Lassie Come Home,* and he told the producer about his own beautiful child.

"We had six little girls lined up who had tried out for *Mrs. Miniver,* and as soon as Elizabeth walked in we sent them all home," Marx said. "It was like an eclipse of the sun. She was wearing a blue velvet cape with a kind of glow of purple about it. We sent her right off to Wardrobe—we didn't even bother to wait for the rushes."

Right from the start Elizabeth exhibited the qualities that were to make her a star. She could memorize

10

pages of dialogue at a glance, needed virtually no rehearsals, and could jump completely into a character from a standstill once the cameras began whirring.

Elizabeth met lifelong friend Roddy McDowall on the set of her first MGM picture, and he fondly remembers the first time he laid eyes on the girl. Cameraman Leonard Smith had glanced at her while bustling around the set and said, "Honey, would you mind going back to the makeup man to have him remove part of your makeup? You have on too much mascara and eye pencil." The girl looked up at him for a heartbeat, then piped up sweetly, "It isn't makeup. It's me!"

*Lassie Come Home* was a hit, and so was Elizabeth. She earned $100 a week as a free-lance actress, and at the end of the film Sara signed her to a $75-a-week contract without any arguments.

The girl dove into a new fairytale life, that of an actress. She wandered around the make-believe streets, parks, lakes, and private zoo located on MGM's 167-acre lot. Between scenes, she attended the required three hours a day of classes in a little red brick schoolhouse. Famous people in fantastic costumes clogged the commissary, nibbling on matzohs and sipping Louis B. Mayer's mother's chicken soup.

Elizabeth made three films during 1944. *Jane Eyre* starring Orson Welles, Joan Fontaine, and Margaret O'Brien was the first. Elizabeth gave a beautiful, tragic performance as Helen Burns, Jane's friend at the orphanage who dies of pneumonia, but years later when she wanted to show her role to her own children, she found that it was cut from the version shown on TV. The second film, *The White Cliffs of Dover* with Irene

Dunne and Alan Marshal, was where she met another lifelong friend for the first time—Peter Lawford.

*National Velvet* was her third film that year—and also the one to launch her as a star. Elizabeth knew the part was perfect for her. "National Velvet was really me," she often says. Her bedroom was decorated with pictures and figurines of horses, saddles, and bridles. She knew how to ride, she was (sort of) British, and she desired that part more than anything else in her whole eleven years.

One problem held her back—she was still as short as a six-year-old, and such a tiny jockey simply wouldn't be convincing on the screen. Although popular myth would have one believe that Elizabeth ate lots of hamburgers and by sheer force of will grew the necessary three inches, producer Pandro S. Berman remembers the incident differently.

"She *had* the part," Berman says. "She was under contract. We had Mickey Rooney lined up. *I* made the decision to wait two years. *I* decided that when she reached a certain height we'd make the picture. And we did."

Two of her baby teeth were pulled so the braces she had to wear for the role would fit properly, but her father balked when the studio wanted to cut her hair also. The legal department researched the problem and decided that she couldn't be forced to cut her hair, so Elizabeth wore a wig.

During the first few years of Elizabeth's career, Francis was forced to put his foot down several times. He refused to let the studio change her name to Virginia, dye her hair, pluck her thick eyebrows, or remove the mole on her cheek that has since become her trademark. Learning early in her career that it wasn't necessary to conform to another's standard of beauty, Elizabeth also resisted MGM's efforts to change her appearance later in life.

Soon after *Velvet* was made, Francis pretty much backed out of his daughter's life. His gallery wasn't doing very well, but his attempts to keep it going consumed most of his time.

Sara, meanwhile, was already on the MGM payroll as Elizabeth's guardian and tutor. Her constant attention to her daughter's career caused her to be called one of the most voracious stage mothers in filmland's history, a woman who was living vicariously through her daughter since her own career had ended prematurely.

Sara vehemently refutes these charges. "It's a lie to say I dominated her in the Hollywood days—we didn't ever want her to be in films. They wanted her for Bonnie in *Gone with the Wind,* and for two years we said 'no.' "

Nevertheless, the Taylors were allowed to spend half of Elizabeth's income, and those thousands of dollars helped the family to maintain their Beverly Hills–fringe life-style. While brother Howard kept a careful distance from the movie madness (even going so far as to shave his head the day before a screen test Sara had arranged), Elizabeth relished her career and did everything her mother suggested to advance it.

Sara even sat behind her daughter's directors, subtly giving signals to improve Elizabeth's performance: she touched her heart if the child needed to put more feeling in the role, she touched her stomach to indicate that Elizabeth's voice was too shrill, or put a plump finger to her lips to cause her daughter to smile more.

Margaret Kerry, Elizabeth's camera double in *Velvet*, remembers cringing every time she heard Sara speak. " 'Oh Elizabeth,' her mother would call out after every scene. 'Oh Elizabeth, darling. Come along.' And Elizabeth, who was very well behaved in those days, would obediently respond, cooing, 'Coming, Mother dear.' "

Not only did *National Velvet* win two Academy Awards, and unanimous accolades for its young star, but it also brought Elizabeth the first trappings of stardom. She was given two horses (one of them *Velvet*'s Pi), a bonus of $15,000, her weekly salary was raised from $200 to $750, and she received $3,000 every time she made a radio appearance. Sara earned $10,000 a year as her daughter's chaperone. The licensing also began: $3,000 for the use of Elizabeth's picture on a Lux soap advertisement, a drawing she did was purchased for $1,000 and put on a greeting card, and Elizabeth Taylor coloring books and paper dolls soon appeared.

A handwritten book by the girl called *Nibbles and Me* —about the live chipmunk she kept in her pocket— was published and sold thousands of copies.

As an adoring public watched, Elizabeth changed from an animal-loving child into a boy-crazy teenager. Her next film, *The Courage of Lassie,* again teamed the child with the popular pooch, but a year later in *Cynthia,* Elizabeth was well on her way to making less well-endowed girls turn green with envy over the way her size thirty-sevens could hold up a strapless gown.

During this time she learned three very important

14

lessons about love, the media, and illness which she would never forget.

The first lesson was that love neither lasts forever, nor does it remain the same. During the filming of *Cynthia* Sara fell in love with the film's director, Michael Curtiz. Francis had slipped further and further out of the female half of his family's celluloid life, and accompanied by his son, he slunk off to Wisconsin to visit Uncle Howard for four months until the storm of passion blew over.

Elizabeth's second lesson was that she attracted a great deal more attention from the world when she was hanging on the arm of a handsome man. It's a well-known secret that the most beautiful girl in America scared off all prospective suitors—for two of her teenage years she couldn't even get a date.

She spent her spare time locked up in her room (which was suddenly redecorated as a surprise by Sara into a green and pink chintz fantasy) writing poetry, drawing, devouring novels, and just staring at the ceiling. Attempting to attract male attention, she took to wearing off-the-shoulder peasant blouses, full skirts tightly cinched in at the waist with wide belts, high heels, and painted her toe- and fingernails fire-engine red.

"I wanted very much to be a part of the real world, which was football games, baseball games, and proms. I was considered a freak by my peers. I never got to do any of that," she says wistfully.

When she turned sixteen the studio raised her salary to $1,000 a week, gave her the beautiful wardrobe of sophisticated clothes she'd worn in *Julia Misbehaves*, and her parents gave her the solid-gold key to a powder-blue Cadillac she wasn't allowed to drive. This began a trend—for many years Elizabeth was content with receiving her wardrobe rather than a raise in pay.

When the friends Howard dutifully dragged home from Beverly Hills High couldn't get up their courage to ask his kid sister out, MGM finally stepped in and began arranging dates for Elizabeth. Her first kiss came from Marshall Thompson, the young star of *The Yearling,* just before Jimmy Lydon brushed her lips on the set of *Cynthia.*

"I just made it under the wire," she now laughs. "Can you imagine anything more humiliating? Being kissed on the screen first before real life!"

After that came the perfect meeting of beauty and brawn. Elizabeth was introduced to the perfect all-American hunk—West Point's football hero Glenn Davis. They shared some ice cream sundaes, played touch football on the beach in front of the Taylors' rented Malibu house, and shared a few passionate kisses when they could sneak away from Sara's watchful scrutiny.

Elizabeth cried bitterly when Davis shipped out to Korea at the summer's end. He left her with his gold football pendant hanging around her neck and the wonderful promise that they were "engaged to be engaged."

After a few months spent filming *The Conspirator* with Robert Taylor in London, the star and her mother met Francis and Howard in Florida to celebrate Elizabeth's seventeenth birthday at a huge bash being thrown by Uncle Howard. Elizabeth expected a grand reunion with Davis, but before he arrived carrying a strand of sixty-nine graduated cultured pearls and an engagement ring, she was introduced to twenty-eight-year-old multimillionaire heir William D. Pawley, Jr.

The tune Pawley squired her around to was far too rich for Davis, and soon after getting his well-publicized welcome-home kiss, he stepped out of the picture, leaving both the pearl necklace and the girl behind.

Elizabeth and Pawley announced their engagement the following May. A three-and-one-half-carat emerald-cut diamond solitaire set with two half-carat diamonds on either side glinted on her finger. "Nice piece of ice. That's what Bill calls it," Elizabeth said, proudly instructing the photogs to include her first diamond in their pix.

The engagement lasted through the star's return to Hollywood to make *The Big Hangover* with Van Johnson, but not much after that. Pawley wanted a little woman whose idea of happiness was hanging around the homestead basking in his glory. Elizabeth swore she was bored stiff with filmmaking and would "much rather make babies," and the "positively drooly" part she was taking in *Father of the Bride* with Spencer Tracy and Joan Bennett would definitely be her last.

MGM, however, chose that moment to send Elizabeth out to Paramount for a plum role, starring with Montgomery Clift and Shelley Winters in *A Place in the Sun.* As desperate as she was to get married, neither the actress nor her mom could pass up a chance for Elizabeth to work with the famous director George Stevens.

Pawley flew to Hollywood in a rage of anger and left

the same way. Elizabeth was only seventeen years old, and her second engagement had just bitten the dust.

Through all these heavings up and down, Elizabeth couldn't help noticing that the media poured gallons of ink into long-winded stories every time she said "I do" or "I don't." In fact, much more space was being devoted to her romances than her movies. Even *Life* magazine had printed a photo of her engagement to Pawley—something national magazines weren't known for back in the '50s.

Since more media exposure equals greater name recognition—which in turn equals bigger box office returns—no one at MGM squawked too loudly about the broken engagements. Although the studio tried desperately to keep their teenage star's reputation squeaky-clean and serene (no smoking, no drinking, and definitely no premarital sex), at the same time the publicists had a little gleam in their eyes about their headline-grabbing gal.

In addition to learning that love never lasts forever, and that romances make splashy headlines, Elizabeth also learned that illness creates sympathy—a fact which would later save her career.

Anytime she had so much as a pimple pop out on her creamy cheek, she was allowed time off from work to seek lotions from a dermatologist. Once she stepped on a nail and was rushed to the infirmary in an ambulance. At the least sign of a sniffle, a doctor was brought on the set. Upon merely mentioning that she felt fatigued, Elizabeth was immediately granted a paid sick day.

Large or small, her health problems demanded attention. When she was working on *A Place in the Sun,*

George Stevens insisted that she spend three days shooting a swimming scene in freezing water when she had bad menstrual cramps. After that she had a stipulation written into all her contracts that she would not work during her period.

Before she was even eighteen, the dye was set for most of the patterns which would haunt Elizabeth's next thirty-three years—the need for the world's attentions, the marriages and subsequent divorces, and the illnesses. All that remained were the drugs and alcohol, and those would come courtesy of her first marriage a few short months later.

# Chapter Two

*"No matter what you or anybody else thinks, I
love this man and I'm going to marry him. I
love him, I love him, I love him."*
—Elizabeth Taylor

THE MGM publicity factory couldn't be happier. For
once they wouldn't have to work their buns off creating a stunt which would focus the media and the public's attention on a new film. The best possible stunt to
publicize their impending *Father of the Bride* was going
to happen a mere month before the movie's release—
the film's star, Elizabeth Taylor, was going to walk
down the aisle in real life.

Unfortunately, the screen marriage of Elizabeth and
Don Taylor was a far greater success than her real
marriage—a mere seven months after radiantly walking down the aisle of the Church of the Good Shep-
herd clutching her father's arm with one hand and her
orchid bouquet with the other, the eighteen-year-old
star found herself a tearful divorcée.

Elizabeth and hotel heir Conrad Nicholson (Nicky)
Hilton had met through Pete Freeman at Paramount
Studios during the fall of 1949. They quickly discovered a shared love for hamburgers, onions, oversized
sweaters, and movies. Their dates often included eve-

nings at the Mocambo together with Sara, Francis, and Nicky's parents, the Conrad Hiltons. Nicky gave her record albums, golf clubs, cashmere sweaters, and, for Christmas, diamond-and-pearl earrings.

With the presentation of a five-carat diamond and a $10,000 platinum-and-diamond wedding band, Elizabeth and Nicky announced their engagement. Their families were thrilled. Sara felt that the Hiltons' wealth brought a fitting upper-class status to her daughter, while Conrad Hilton (who had already shown his rapture with Hollywood by marrying Zsa Zsa Gabor) felt that Elizabeth's world-famous name only enhanced his own.

Even though close friends such as Montgomery Clift asked Elizabeth if it was wise to be taking such a big step so young, she assured everyone that Nicky was definitely the man of her dreams and she knew perfectly well what she was doing. She loved the idea of getting married, and once the presents began rolling in, she felt positive that she was making the right move.

"I thought I was in love," she said decades later. "I thought marriage was a cottage with a white picket fence and roses climbing over it. I was unprepared for that world out there. I'd been so sheltered by my family, the studio. I was no more grown up than a little animal."

Elizabeth's wedding was possibly the biggest in Hollywood's history. MGM's present was the $3,500 gown commissioned by Helen Rose, the six yellow organdy bridesmaids' dresses, and Sara's bronze chiffon mother-of-the-bride outfit. Elizabeth's going-away ensemble was designed by Edith Head and donated by

Paramount. Ceil Chapman of New York sent her trousseau. After she posed with their products, the Gorham Silver Company gave her a forty-five-piece silver service. Conrad Hilton gave the young couple 100 shares of Hilton Hotel stock (valued at only $1,350 at the time, but worth $150,000 thirty years later). Uncle Howard Young gave the bride a $65,000 pearl ring. Friends threw her several showers and gave her beautiful presents of lingerie.

"I just love everything about getting married," Elizabeth said at the time, "and every little detail seems terribly important to me."

On Saturday, May 6, 1950, the church was overflowing with Tinsel Town's elite. Nearly everyone who worked at MGM had been invited, and the celebrities included Janet Leigh, Spencer Tracy, Rosalind Russell, Fred Astaire, Ginger Rogers, Debbie Reynolds, Gene Kelly, Greer Garson, Zsa Zsa Gabor, Esther Williams, June Allyson, and Dick Powell. Between 2,500 and 3,500 gawkers, and hundreds of members of the press, waited outside the church to catch a glimpse of the happy couple.

And, perhaps, the crowd was witnessing the only time they were a happy couple—their kiss lasted so long that Monsignor Patrick J. Cancannon was forced to intercede.

For hours on end, six hundred people kissed the dewy-eyed bride as she personally thanked them for their kind gifts, then the guests congratulated her impatient husband on their way into the reception. For the first time in her life, Elizabeth found it was easier to keep her personality cheerfully sparkling after polishing off a couple of glasses of the bubbly. It made her feel light and grand, and was a definite help in getting her through the exhausting day.

*En route* to Europe aboard the *Queen Mary*, Elizabeth and Nicky dined with the Duke and Duchess of Windsor. A brand-new Cadillac—to better tour the Continent—had been brought on board with their luggage. Yet, despite the first-class voyage, the dream marriage quickly turned into a nightmare during the honeymoon.

Every place the couple went, they were mobbed with fans wanting to take the actress's photo and get her autograph. Well-indoctrinated MGM girl that she was, sometimes she spent up to two hours signing and posing.

"I didn't marry a girl, I married an institution," Hilton grumbled.

To get even, Nicky spent night after night gambling recklessly in the casinos of Monte Carlo and France, leaving underage Elizabeth sitting alone and waiting. He slept until late in the afternoon when she wanted to explore all the exciting side streets, historical sites, and shops. She adored making love with him and would hug and nuzzle him at every opportunity, but friends they met during the honeymoon said he would push her away in disgust, saying he was "goddammed sick and tired of looking" at her face. Crying her eyes out, Elizabeth ran away and would spend the night curled up on a couch in a friend's room. She began chain-smoking during this time in a vain attempt to calm her nerves.

A friend who had lunch with Elizabeth in New York after she returned from the five-month sojourn said the actress showed up wearing a long-sleeved blouse with a high neck. As the actress cried out her pain and sorrow over her husband's callous treatment, her friend spied welts and bruises all over her arms through the blouse's thin fabric. When Elizabeth fainted on the set of *Father's Little Dividend* and was brought home in the midst of a miscarriage, Nicky coolly kissed her, said he'd be back in a few days, and went on his planned fishing trip.

Elizabeth fumed, fought, and finally fled. Despite cajoling from her mother that she try to patch things up, the actress temporarily moved in with girlfriend Marjorie Dillon, issued a press release beginning "I am sorry that Nicky and I are unable to adjust our differences and that we have come to a final parting of the ways," and filed for divorce.

Aghast at her audacity, the Hiltons counted every sheet and towel to make sure that Elizabeth didn't get more than her share. Adding insult to injury, MGM even demanded that she and her bridesmaids return their gowns.

Stressed to the limit, Elizabeth suffered an emotional collapse and checked into Cedars of Lebanon Hospital under the name of Rebecca Jones, for a week of kindly ministrations.

A few days later, on January 29, 1951, a thin, pale, and trembling Elizabeth told Judge Thurmond Clarke in a tiny, quavering voice how her husband "was indifferent to me and used abusive language." The twenty-minute divorce proceeding was as long as her marriage ceremony had been.

Now a free woman who had to decide what to do with her life, Elizabeth moved into a five-room apartment on Wilshire Boulevard, upstairs from Tony Cur-

tis and Janet Leigh. Neither she nor roommate/
companion Peggy Rutledge could cook, which didn't
matter much because Elizabeth had been put on a diet
of baby food since her raw nerves had affected her
digestion. Work was the best cure for what ailed her,
the studio decided.

Sniffing out her loneliness, the potential suitors immediately moved in. One man, though immensely
wealthy and powerful, was simply too unsavory for
Elizabeth's tastes. Nevertheless, Howard Hughes tried
every trick in his well-armed arsenal to get the actress
to like him after spotting her back in 1948 when he was
using a pay phone in the lobby of the Beverly Hills
Hotel. Hughes immediately sent his lackey to find out
where the beauty was going, and discovered she was
the art-gallery owner's daughter.

After purchasing two paintings from Francis, he
asked the Taylors (and their gorgeous daughter) out
to dinner. In the weeks that followed, Hughes took the
Taylors to Reno for a weekend and beseeched Hollywood's hostesses to invite them both to dinner parties.
Once Elizabeth got wind of his conniving, she began
fending off invitations with "If Howard is coming, I'm
not."

Hughes had gotten the hint after Elizabeth announced her engagement to Bill Pawley, but resur-
faced with even more ardent wooing after she
divorced Hilton—he promised her one million dollars
if she'd consent to marry him.

Elizabeth refused, saying, "He was such an out-and-
out bore I wouldn't have married him for all his
money." She said Hughes seemed scatterbrained and
never responded to questions she asked him. Plus, his

personal appearance disgusted her. "He often looked like he needed a bath. Whenever I saw him, his pants were wrinkled and hanging on him like a tent, and sometimes he wore dirty sneakers with no socks and his toes sticking out of holes."

A much more desirable beau turned up in the form of the director of her next movie, *Love is Better than Ever* —Stanley Donen. Elizabeth appeared at the benefit premiere of *Father's Little Dividend* hanging on Donen's arm; soon after Jeanne Donen filed for divorce.

Finished with her work on *Love*, Elizabeth had plenty of time to entertain Korean War vets and be escorted around town by Donen. MGM didn't approve of this scandalous pairing in the least, and quickly shipped the protesting young woman off to England to play in *Ivanhoe* opposite Robert Taylor and Joan Fontaine.

Not only was *Ivanhoe* a movie Elizabeth did not want to make, playing a part she had no interest in, but there were other reasons she wanted to remain in the States. The first, naturally, was to be with Donen. Also, her brother Howard had just received his draft notice and was moving his wedding to Mara Regan up to June 23 so they could be wed before he joined the service.

All Elizabeth's pleas were in vain. She couldn't even refuse to do the film and take a suspension, because that would mean no salary. No longer a cossetted little girl, the self-supporting woman forced herself to take the role, but never promised anyone she'd do a good job at it. The petulant child in her gave one of her worst film performances with a blank face, slack jaw, and indifferent speeches. All her dialogue had to be re-recorded back in Hollywood and dubbed in later.

Just before things got horribly unbearable, Cupid came to her rescue. England suddenly became merry when she was reacquainted with Michael Wilding, the leading romantic British star at that time, whom Elizabeth had developed a crush on while making *The Conspirator* three years earlier.

"Rather than ask the waitress for some salt, that Taylor chit will walk clear through the commissary to get it from the kitchen, wiggling her hips," Wilding told Stewart Granger at the time. "Then she wiggles her way back again, past my table."

Wilding first asked out the black-haired beauty and her companion Peggy because "I honestly thought she might be lonely." After a few dates, Peggy stopped tagging along.

Before long Elizabeth bought herself an enormous diamond-studded sapphire ring and proposed to an actor twenty years her senior. Explaining her actions, Elizabeth said, "He was everything I wanted in a man, and I thought him remarkable."

Stalling for time, while continuing to see his own idol and beloved friend—forty-seven-year-old Marlene Dietrich—Wilding told Elizabeth she was too young for him. He was not living with his wife, but had yet to get a divorce. Vacillating between these three women for a time, Wilding finally chose the young beauty who chased him down relentlessly.

"Elizabeth wants to be married to someone who will love and protect her, and that someone, by some heaven-sent luck, turns out to be me," he told the press while their friends giggled behind their hands at the way Elizabeth mothered him.

On February 21, 1952, at the Caxton Hall Registry

Office in London, a bemused Wilding wed a glowing Tayor resplendent in a dove-gray Helen Rose suit. Friends who had recently seen how vivacious the actor was with Marlene Dietrich and how bored he had looked earlier the same night with Elizabeth wondered what he was getting himself into.

For better and for worse, for richer and for poorer, the couple remained together for five years and produced two sons, Michael and Christopher.

Right from the beginning, the richer and poorer part posed a problem with the Wildings. Michael wondered how he would pay for their honeymoon, so Elizabeth picked up the tab. When they returned to Hollywood, her contract with MGM was about to expire, and business associates were pushing her to consider becoming a free agent—thus gaining the opportunities to call her own shots for both money and roles. But, Wilding didn't have any work to look forward to and had to pay about $100,000 in British taxes.

Elizabeth signed a five-year contract with MGM for $5,000 a week and an additional $300 for Sara Taylor. Wilding was offered a three-year $3,000-a-week contract containing an option of an additional two years at $4,000 a week. Although it sounds like a tremendous amount of money, even today, it was only paid for a forty-week year, and the studio always reserved the right to lay off actors at whim.

Although the couple intended to live simply in Elizabeth's apartment, she quickly got pregnant and wanted the baby to grow up in a house. Perched on a hilltop, the $75,000 home was called "too bloody expensive" by Wilding. Elizabeth floated a $50,000 loan from MGM and bought furniture with the $46,000 that had been held in reserve from her childhood earnings.

Happy that at long last she had found true love and was to experience motherhood, Elizabeth allowed herself to indulge in whatever tasty tidbits she wanted. As her weight ballooned up forty-three pounds from her normally petite 112, MGM decided she was unphotographable and suspended her at a reduced salary of $2,000 a week.

"You would have thought I was the only woman who ever conceived and carried a child," she says. "Indulging in all my pregnant whims, I ended up weighing 150 pounds. And the bigger I got, the more benign and happy I got, like a big momma."

After Michael Howard was born by cesarean section on January 6, 1953, Elizabeth was kept on her reduced pay because MGM deemed that she was still too fat to play the lead roles in *All the Brothers Were Valiant* and *Young Bess.* After a crash diet she described as "coffee for breakfast, eggs for lunch, and steak for dinner— with pink grapefruit coming out of my ears," brought her weight down to a reasonable 117, the studio lent her out to Paramount to star opposite Dana Andrews and Peter Finch in *Elephant Walk,* taking over a role that Vivien Leigh was unable to complete because she had suffered a nervous breakdown.

As the years went by, Elizabeth found herself shouldering more and more of the family's financial burden. Michael liked to stay home and dabble at painting rather than hustle for jobs at the studio. He refused many roles, including one opposite Grace Kelly in *The*

*Swan* and Rex Harrison's role in *My Fair Lady.* "I was just too lazy to do them," he said.

The Wildings' enormous expenses continued to pile up. Her hobbies were—by her own admission—"clothes and jewels," but since her husband couldn't afford the gems she picked out, she'd produce the cash herself. Their mortgage and loan payments all had to be paid monthly, as did the salaries of Peggy Rutledge (Elizabeth's personal secretary), a cook, maid, gardener, and nanny. On top of that was food for their menagerie: four dogs, five cats, and two ducks.*

"She hangs her things up on the floor," Wilding moaned. "Any floor. She can make a room look more like a typhoon hit it than a typhoon would." Although displeased that his wife couldn't cook more than bacon and eggs that soon turned cold because she'd forgotten to warm the plates, he didn't exactly get off his duff to help her.

Although Wilding lazed around the pool all day, Elizabeth was churning out film after film. *Rhapsody, Beau Brummel, The Girl Who Had Everything, Elephant Walk,* and *The Last Time I Saw Paris* were all made between 1953 and '54.

Her next film—*Giant*—came four months after son Christopher was born (also through a painful cesarean), and was again directed by George Stevens. The only similarity to *A Place in the Sun* was that both films were nominated for most of the top Academy Awards, and each time only Stevens' direction brought home the statuette. Elizabeth's role was one of her

* One writer who interviewed Elizabeth at home was aghast at how the cats had shredded the woven grass wallpaper, and how the dogs used any available floor space to relieve themselves.

most demanding to date: the film spans thirty years, and her character ages from an innocent young bride to a gray-haired grandmother.

Not only did *Giant* mark one of Elizabeth's greatest film roles, it was also a turning point in her life. Although everyone in Hollywood, including Gary Cooper, wanted the lead role, Stevens chose Rock Hudson. When he asked Hudson whom he wanted for his wife in the film, Hudson chose Elizabeth over Grace Kelly "because she had such an incredible beauty."

Elizabeth was the only one on the set who made friends with the third star—James Dean. At twenty-four, he was only a year older than she, and Elizabeth was able to ignore his eccentricities like wearing the same shirt every day after work for three weeks without washing it. When he finished his scenes before the rest of the stars, Elizabeth gave him a Siamese kitten as a going-away present.

Four days later, speeding through the intersection of Highways 466 and 41 near Paso Robles, California, Dean sent his silver Porsche Spyder smashing into the side of a Ford and was killed instantly.

Overwhelmed by grief, Elizabeth spat fire at Stevens, who insisted that she act on the day following Dean's death. Unsatisfied with her work, he demanded that she reshoot the scene the next day; but instead the actress was rushed to the UCLA Medical Center suffering from acute abdominal pains which turned out to be a twisted colon. Two weeks later, when she'd recovered sufficiently to be released, *Giant* had wrapped.

Elizabeth's rapidly crumbling marriage only increased her stress. Hudson often stayed up nights listening to his friend weep about her fear of another divorce and the thought of being alone again. While she was telling him that their marriage "had become the relationship for which we were much more suited —brother and sister," Wilding was despondent about how dependent he'd become on his young wife in recent years.

Again clinging to her friend Montgomery Clift for moral support, Elizabeth began filming *Raintree County* with him. But Monty had problems of his own. After leaving a dull dinner party at the Wildings one evening, which included gallons of warm rosé and two downers he'd popped on the way, he wrapped his car around a telephone pole.

Rock Hudson, another dinner guest, remembered how Clift was spitting out teeth and oozing blood all over Elizabeth's silk dress as she cradled his head. "It took forever for the doctor to come—forever," he said. Elizabeth fended off the inevitable photographers by screaming: "You son of a bitch! I'll kick you in the nuts! If you dare take a picture of him like this, I'll never let you near me again. Get out of here, you fucking bastards!" then rode in the ambulance to the hospital with her friend.

The film was postponed for two months as Clift slowly attempted to drag himself back to health. Not long after the incident, his self-destructive side overtook him again. A few months later he tried to O.D. on sleeping pills, and on two different nights the dazed actor was discovered on the streets of *Raintree*'s location of Danville, Kentucky, wearing only his birthday suit.

But as bad as life seemed, just before beginning *Cat on a Hot Tin Roof*, Elizabeth managed to find something to purr about: his name was Mike Todd.

Todd was her knight in shining armor—the man who knew how to indulge her every whim and fantasy while still keeping her in line. He respected her brains, her talent, and her body—something no other man had done. He awoke the passion in her and showed her just how large the world could be once she removed her blinders.

An incredible showman and entrepreneur who had owned his own two-million-dollars-a-year contracting business at age eighteen, was dead broke a year later, earned another fortune soundproofing the stages in Hollywood, lost the money during the Depression, and regained it with his invention of the Todd-AO camera, Todd was finishing up his grand accomplishment *Around the World in 80 Days* when he invited the Wildings to spend a weekend on a yacht party hosted by himself and live-in lover Evelyn Keyes during the summer of 1956.

A miserable Elizabeth drank champagne nonstop all weekend to forget that she and Wilding were on the brink of announcing their separation, and acted somewhat obnoxious.

She chalked up the cold shoulder her host gave her to his legendary hatred of both actresses and women who drink. She knew that he was twenty-three years older than she, had a son two years her senior, and that his first wife had died under mysterious circumstances, while his second—Joan Blondell—left him after he borrowed her life savings, then went bankrupt ten weeks after their wedding.

Yet the day after she and Wilding announced their impending divorce, Todd phoned that he just had to see her, dragged her into an empty office in the Thalberg Building, and urgently told her that she had better get used to the idea that he was going to be her next husband. Elizabeth left with her head spinning and later told a friend that before that day "we had never touched hands."

He pursued her with the unstinting energy he showed everything in his life—showering her with flowers every day on the set of *Raintree County,* flying her to Chicago one day for lunch, meeting her for romantic weekends, and taking her to New York on shopping sprees, where he introduced her to friends as "my fat little Jewish broad, Lizzie Schwartzkopf."

"He called me every night [during the six weeks on location]," Elizabeth says. "We got to know each other on the phone."

Before they were engaged over Labor Day weekend, 1956, he had given her a $30,000 pearl friendship ring "for weekdays," and she was by his side the night his grand accomplishment, *Around the World in 80 Days,* opened. Right after the premiere, he gave her a 29.7-carat diamond engagement ring valued at $92,000.

Less than a month later she slipped when coming down a staircase on a yacht, and the resulting crushed spinal discs forced her to spend six weeks at the Harkness Pavilion of Columbia-Presbyterian Medical Center in New York. The three crushed discs were removed and replaced during a five-hour operation with bones taken from her hip, pelvis, and a bone bank.

Sometimes Elizabeth would "burn up with pain and

black out" because the doctors refused to give her the massive doses of drugs necessary to block out her agony. Upon learning that she was pregnant, her doctors tried unsuccessfully to convince her to have an abortion, insisting that having a baby so soon after the back surgery could be fatal.

Wanting to cheer her up, Todd brought by a few little distractions: a Renoir, a Monet, a Pissarro, and a Frans Hals to decorate the walls Elizabeth described as painted a "pale vomit green."

He bought her a Rolls-Royce and a yacht to help speed her recovery, and convinced Michael Wilding to join them in Acapulco to expedite a quickie divorce. Elizabeth and Todd wed on February 2, 1957—the day after her divorce was granted—in a seaside villa decorated with 1500 white gladioli and sixty bushels of white orchids, guarded by armed members of the Mexican Army.

Francis and Sara flew in from Hollywood; Michael Todd, Jr., Eddie Fisher, and Mexican singer Cantinflas were Todd's attendants; sister-in-law Mara and Debbie Reynolds were the bridesmaids. Elizabeth, looking trim, tan, and utterly blissful in a low-cut pale blue Helen Rose dress, was characteristically an hour late for the ceremony and already tipsy from the several glasses of champagne she used to anesthetize her back pain.

She felt that "This marriage will last forever. For me it will be the third time lucky." Francis told reporters he wished her all the happiness in the world, adding, "I hope that this time her dreams will come true."

Her dreams did come true, but only for a tragically short time. Todd died a fiery death while flying to New

York in a plane he'd named *The Lucky Liz,* with a photo of his wife tucked into his pocket. But the Todds had a wonderful marriage.

He gave her a present every Saturday to commemorate the day they first met—hats, couturier gowns, ruby necklaces, diamond earrings, a diamond tiara, sapphires, emeralds, and sometimes just a lipstick. On her twenty-fifth birthday, she was delighted to unwrap a diamond bracelet, a mink coat, and a Renoir. For their six-month anniversary he offered her a choice between two mink coats—one a diadem, the other a diamond. After careful consideration, she chose them both.

On the following August 6, Elizabeth was tended by eight doctors who delivered her first daughter—a beautiful child called Elizabeth Frances and known always as Liza.

Everything the Todds did was passionate, from their shocking kiss before the prime minister of Australia to their ear-shattering, profanity-spiked public brawls. When he won an Oscar for *Around the World,* he refused to stop kissing her long enough for the photogs to shoot a frontal portrait of him.

While traveling the world to promote the film, Elizabeth fell ill in Hong Kong and decided to return to California to have her appendix removed—even though the organ wasn't infected. She forced Todd to take the hotel room next to her own and stay there— without a phone—to get a little time alone with him.

In the end, it was actually Elizabeth's poor health that saved her life. Never apart from Todd for even one night, Elizabeth was forced to stay home the night he left for New York to accept the Showman-of-the-

Year award from the Friars Club. She was suffering from bronchitis and had a temperature of 102°. He had already waited three days for her condition to improve. There was a storm in Los Angeles when he left, and he promised to call her as soon as he landed to refuel. Todd rushed back into the bedroom five times to say good-bye, and the couple clung together for long minutes before he walked out the door.

Elizabeth didn't sleep all night, and when his call didn't come, she immediately knew something was wrong. But she didn't hear the official news until the next morning. The only identifiable piece of Todd recovered from the wreck was his twisted, blackened wedding ring.

"Oh, God! No! No! It can't be! No! God, I can't live without him!" The screams tore through the home on Schuyler Road in Beverly Hills that Elizabeth had shared with Todd. It was March 23, 1958—they'd been married ten days short of fourteen months.

"I have never seen anyone so grief-stricken," said Helen Rose. "Her whole life seemed to have come apart, and there were no words of comfort."

As the grief seared through the young woman, her friends and family quickly gathered around, but there was nothing anyone could say or do to help ease her pain. Her physician, Dr. Rex Kennamer, kept her heavily sedated during the following weeks, and friends at the funeral in Zurich, Illinois, said the actress had to be propped up by her secretary Dick Hanley and Dr. Kennamer.

Two thousand people turned out on the freezing day Mike Todd was laid to rest. They were picnicking among the graves, babies crawling all over the tombstones. "Liz, Liz," they screamed when she stepped out of her limo hanging on to her brother's arm. After the ceremony, the horde rushed at her, ripping at her clothing for souvenirs. The crowd around her car was so thick that the driver couldn't climb in for ten minutes.

This was just the beginning of the hellish weeks in store for Elizabeth. Surrounded by her memories of what could have been, she sobbed nonstop. She got into the habit of popping a pill to make her body do the things she knew it needed to do—sleep, wake up, calm down. All she'd eat was bowls of popcorn washed down with Coors beer straight from the can. She slept in a shirt Todd had worn just before leaving, refused to change the sheets, and kept his pajamas next to her in bed. She wore his blackened wedding ring next to her own.

"I want to die," she kept saying. "I just want to die."

What finally brought Elizabeth back into the land of the living was the thing that reminded her the most of Todd—her work. She'd begun the role of Maggie in *Cat on a Hot Tin Roof* before the crash. At that time Elizabeth vowed that it would be her second-to-last movie—once her contract was up, she had planned to retire and be a housewife.

Before his death, Todd had said the role was meant for her—she'd be fantastic. So Elizabeth again flung herself into her work as a means of forgetting pain, and was soon working with an energy she didn't know she possessed.

She often ran off the set in tears and had many sick days when she couldn't bear to face the cameras, but in between it all she turned in a stellar performance.

Never one to rehearse, she could immediately jump into character when director Richard Brooks signaled "action," often leaving dumbfounded co-star Paul Newman in the dust.

"Elizabeth . . . has got a hell of a lot more talent than most people give her credit for," Newman said at the time. Burl Ives echoed his co-star's thoughts: "She's the best of the bunch."

Although still deeply mourning her husband, Elizabeth hated to be alone and began dating a few months after Todd's funeral. She was often spotted out on the town with Arthur Loew, Jr. But it was her first public appearance after Todd's death which gave the world any foreshadowing of the riveting headlines down the road: Elizabeth innocently accompanied Debbie Reynolds to a ringside seat at the Tropicana in Las Vegas where the blonde actress's husband—Eddie Fisher— was opening his show.

Just who chased whom has remained a hotly contested matter. Fisher had looked up to Mike Todd as his mentor, and from watching their marriage he already knew Elizabeth "could be a spoiled brat," but he also felt sorry for her.

"Her beauty was a curse," Fisher said. "Fighting to prove she was an actress . . . had made her tough. She could drink with the best of them; she swore; she was the antithesis of her ethereal, ladylike screen image. Yet she was also timid, insecure, and vulnerable, a little girl trapped inside a woman's body."

Glamorous Elizabeth was also the total antithesis of his own wife with her studied sweetness, thrifty ways, and homemade dresses. The marriage of Eddie Fisher and Debbie Reynolds was already on the rocks when

39

they attended the Todds' wedding. Neither had been sure of their own joining, but both had felt compelled to marry because of the unbelievable mountain of publicity which started their family, friends, and fans clamoring for the event. Fisher and Reynolds were both seeing psychiatrists to help them through the pain of a divorce that conservative, moralistic Reynolds was fighting tooth and nail.

Though the blonde star did every conceivable thing a woman can to try to keep her man—including getting pregnant—Fisher was captivated by the flash and excitement of Elizabeth. In turn, the dark-haired beauty reveled in the way the singer catered to her physical and emotional ailments while providing a last link to Todd.

What began as the casual meetings of two friends to mourn a shared loved one soon turned into a raging passion. Nothing could keep Elizabeth and Fisher apart—they began dating publicly and were soon openly living together.

The social mores of 1958 being what they were, these actions—especially coming mere months after Mike Todd's death—immediately branded Elizabeth as a scarlet woman in the public's eye. And since the sordid details about Fisher and Reynolds' marital problems had not been made public at that time, Elizabeth's moral indiscretions also included breaking up that decade's perfect all-American family.

Elizabeth was still under contract, so there was no problem getting work, but appalled fans—shocked by her scandalous behavior—turned away from her in droves.

A defiant Elizabeth didn't care a whit about public

opinion. She had long ago tired of being the obedient little girl who automatically did whatever she was told. In fact, all the adverse publicity may have actually caused her to flaunt her love more aggressively while intensifying her desire for a quick marriage.

Defeated, Reynolds finally permitted a Nevada divorce, and an ecstatic Elizabeth stayed with Fisher throughout his six-week Las Vegas booking which was just long enough to establish residency allowing him to duck out of his marriage.

Three hours after his divorce was final, Fisher married Elizabeth under a traditional Jewish chuppah, a canopy decorated with carnations and gardenias. The bride appeared only a half hour late this time, wearing a gorgeous Jean Louis–designed moss-green chiffon dress.

Just as traditionally, the newly converted Jewish princess told the press that she and husband number four would "be on our honeymoon for thirty or forty years" and immediately announced her plans to retire from films.

Like Todd, Fisher loved showering her with the jewels that made her eyes sparkle. But gems weren't the cement needed to glue together a marriage on shaky grounds from the beginning. Elizabeth once confided to friend and lover Max Lerner, the political columnist, that by marrying Fisher, "I thought I could keep Mike's memory alive, but I have only his ghost."

Years later she said her relationship with Fisher had been "sick."

Elizabeth's eight weeks of work on her next film, *Suddenly Last Summer,* brought her a $500,000 paycheck —and made her the highest-paid actress in the world.

41

It reunited her with friend Montgomery Clift, as well as giving her the opportunity to work with Katharine Hepburn. Constantly entwined in Eddie's arms, she announced that her next picture would be *Cleopatra* for 20th Century Fox, and she'd only do it for one million long green dollar bills. Fox figured that having the famous star playing the role of the famous vixen would bring the ailing studio back to life. Elizabeth's salary was the largest in the history of films up to that point, and for a long time after.

Before that, MGM reminded Elizabeth not too subtly that she still had to do one film under her old contract for the paltry sum of $125,000. If she refused to play the call girl in *Butterfield 8*, they would suspend her without pay and could legally prevent her from working for another film company for two years.

Since she and Fisher had some expensive bills to pay and Reynolds was getting the bulk of his money, Elizabeth could hardly refuse the role; but she wasn't shy about telling anyone who would listen how much she abhorred the role. "The leading lady is almost a prostitute. She's a sick nymphomaniac," Elizabeth said.

Though she threatened to wreak more than her usual accidental havoc and destruction upon the set, producer Pandro Berman told her: "Just play the part and you'll get the Academy Award."

Although she managed to finagle the role of the piano player for her husband (and was terribly disgruntled when most of it ended up on the cutting-room floor), she never stopped telling the press "I hate the girl I play. I don't like what she stands for— the men, the sleeping around."

Of course, Berman was right about the award.

When Yul Brynner announced that she'd won the Best Actress Oscar for 1960, she looked fittingly surprised; but she has always remained firmly convinced that the statue was only given to her out of sympathy after she nearly died.

After finally completing *Butterfield,* Elizabeth and Fisher flew to London for the filming of *Cleopatra.* The delays in the shooting were ridiculous and a bored Elizabeth got sick. Her case of Asian flu worsened to the point of acute staphylococcus pneumonia.

By the time she was rushed to the hospital with a high fever and wheeled into the operating room for the emergency tracheotomy necessary for her to breathe, the doctors thought she had less than an hour to live. She remembers that she couldn't breathe and lapsed into a coma several times.

The public hung on to her every rasping breath. Every turn of her condition made the headlines. When a weak, but still living Elizabeth tottered up to the stage to fetch her statue—the bandage from her tracheotomy scar still wound around her neck—the world shared her tears of joy. Nearly dying brought back all the fans who had deserted her just before she married Fisher. The sympathy created by her illness had made her a bigger star than ever before.

No longer was she labeled a scarlet woman, a homewrecker. Somehow she'd transcended the realm of mere mortal film actress and was allowed into the hallowed gates of celestial stardom.

By the time Elizabeth returned to the *Cleopatra* set, it had moved from London to Rome and had a complete new lineup of male stars, because the previous ones had gone on to other commitments. Her script was bound in moroccan leather, and an entire building on the studio lot was dubbed "Casa Taylor" and converted into a dressing room for her. Twentieth Century Fox had already spent six months and five million dollars shooting ten minutes of footage they had to scrap and would end up spending $500,000 a week on the film until it added up to the incredible sum of forty million dollars.

Perhaps some people went to see *Cleopatra* because of the story; maybe some saw it because of the lavish costumes and set designs; but most people flooded into the theaters to see the red-hot couple who created the headlines they'd been reading about in all the newspapers and magazines.

Elizabeth's new leading man, Richard Burton, replaced not only Stephen Boyd as Marc Antony, but also Eddie Fisher as Elizabeth's love interest by the end of the movie.

The mating of Elizabeth Taylor with Richard Burton was an event decreed by some unknown fate—like two planets colliding. Though each had been warned that the other was predatory, sexually irresistible, and publicity hungry, both of them laughed in their detractors' faces and established their own undefeatable strength and power.

While publicly proclaiming nothing of the sort would ever happen, Elizabeth and Burton fell for each other hard, fast, and completely. Their love affair makes one understand that a cliche like "This is bigger than the both of us" has its root in reality.

From the excessive bouts of drinking where wooden-legged Elizabeth matched bottomless-pit Burton gulp for gulp, to the extravagant jewels worth a king's ransom that he bestowed upon her, to the earth-shaking shrieking matches and earth-moving loving reconciliations—everything about their romance was the stuff legends (and headlines) are made of.

Elizabeth may have thought that Burton—with his strong will that alternated from gallant to abusive—would be another mentor/father/lover as Mike Todd had been. But, though they loved hard and fought hard, in the end their relationship was destructive to each of them personally and to the two of them as a couple.

Elizabeth and Fisher were in the process of adopting Maria—a little handicapped German child—and the actress had just turned thirty years old when what Burton called *"Le Scandale"* erupted. Headlines like "Liz, Burton go arm-in-arm on all-night Roman date" and "Liz and Burton frolic in Rome; kiss, dance" jumped onto newspapers around the world. Despite condemnation from the world press, the public, and even the Vatican; and perhaps most of all, despite Eddie Fisher's love, devotion, and wracking pain —Elizabeth divorced him on March 6, 1964. The long-suffering Sybil Burton had finally caved in the previous December, divorcing her husband of fourteen years and the father of her two children.

Nine days after her divorce was final from Fisher, Elizabeth was married to Burton in Montreal. By the time they were divorced for the second time in July of 1976, Elizabeth was forty-four years old, miserable, chunky, and clinging to a dying relationship with Henry Wynberg, the used-car salesman who had comforted her so well after her first split from Burton.

By the mid 70's, one might have thought that Elizabeth had conquered all the mountains she could: she had already been a reigning queen of several scandals, had broken box office records all over the world, received two Academy Awards, been married to five famous/wealthy/handsome/powerful men, had four lovely children, and owned one of the most fabulous jewelry and art collections on the globe.

Yet, there was still one arena she had barely grazed in passing, one which was panting for her presence and would soon embrace her with open arms—the Washington political scene.

She had flitted through a few times before—notably on the arm of wealthy Iranian Ambassador Ardeshir Zahedi—and even endorsed Jimmy Carter during his bid for president, but never stayed long. Then in July 1976, she was escorted to a Bicentennial dinner by the handsome, silver-haired former secretary of the navy, John Warner. He was a gentleman farmer with an income left over after his divorce settlement from heiress Catherine Mellon.

Warner swept Elizabeth down to his 2,700-acre farm in Virginia and off her feet. Her misery over losing Burton to young, beautiful Susan Hunt, and her humiliation over the way Henry Wynberg had ordered her out of the house they had shared in Beverly Hills, was over. The farm "reminds me of my childhood home in England," she told her new beau.

Warner proposed on a grass-covered hillside as an electrical storm raged around them, sending down torrents of rain and zigzags of lightning in every direction. They were married on the same hilltop the following December 4. She was finally going to throw off all her trappings of stardom and be "just a wife," content to stay home on the farm and fry up some chicken, wearing her Halston caftan.

Then Warner announced that he intended to seek a seat in the senate, and the formerly Democratic Elizabeth threw herself into the Republican waters as enthusiastically as the Christian Science Elizabeth had thrown herself into Catholicism before marrying Nicky Hilton and into Judaism during her marriages to Mike Todd and Eddie Fisher.

She kissed babies, attended rallies, and choked on chicken bones in tiny hamlets from one end of Virginia to the other. "If John wants to campaign as a candidate, I'll be with him all the way side by side," she said. "I love Washington and Virginia. I am not intimidated by politics. I think it's fascinating."

Apparently, something was still missing from her life, and she was filling that gap with food. "I'd like to be a hausfrau, and then I could eat as much as I want and drink as much as I want," she told a reporter, and it looked as though she'd finally gotten her wish.

By the time Warner was sworn into office, her noshing on chili dogs, popcorn, French fries, and chocolate bars had ballooned her up to nearly 175 pounds. One Washington matron was overheard sighing, "All our lives we have wanted to look like Elizabeth Taylor, and now—God help us—we do."

All the while espousing how much she loved being down on the farm, Elizabeth continued making films— most of them bad ones. After having made critically acclaimed films with Burton such as *Who's Afraid of Virginia Woolf?* (for which she received her second Best Actress award) and *The Taming of the Shrew,* she now found herself in dogs like *A Little Night Music, The Blue Bird, Ash Wednesday,* and cameo roles in disappointing works such as *Winter Kills.*

Her life was at an ebb. Despite constant bouts of exercise and dieting at luxury spas, her weight continued to yo-yo up and down drastically. When she complained about the agony of her back pain, friends suggested that swimming in Warner's pool would help to alleviate the pain. Bitterly explaining that her husband was too cheap to heat the water, she'd pop another of the pain pills that were so readily available. Although she told pals she could stop drinking whenever she wanted to, somehow that desire never came.

Things began to look up slightly when she slimmed down enough to look ravishing in her stage debut playing Regina Giddens in *The Little Foxes.* She was terrific, and so were the reviews in Washington and New York. But, by the time she took the play to London and Los Angeles, several discouraging words were being bandied about.

In December 1981, Elizabeth and Warner announced their separation. In two short months she'd be fifty, and she still hadn't found the love and happiness she had wanted for her entire life. Instead, she was filling in the cracks with excessive amounts of food, alcohol, and pain-killers.

# Chapter Three

*"Hello, my name is Elizabeth. I'm an addict and an alcoholic."*—Elizabeth Taylor

By the time Elizabeth announced her separation from John Warner, an interesting transformation had taken place. In photos taken around the time of their marriage, Elizabeth is looking frankly old and dumpy—her eyes lost in rolls of fat, her thick thighs bulging from a slit in her too tight dress, and what Joan Rivers called "more chins than a Hong Kong phone book" hung in folds around her neck—while Warner looks sleekly slim and boyishly handsome. Five years later Elizabeth has regained her svelte and sparkling looks, and it is Warner who is sporting flaps of flesh under his jaw, tired, puffy eyes, and silver hair that no longer looks dashing.

Dr. Joyce Brothers swiftly published an article in *Good Housekeeping* explaining "Why Elizabeth Taylor Can't Stay Married." She prophesied that, unlike the rest of us who can get a lift from simply buying a new pair of shoes or an outfit, Elizabeth can afford anything in the world, so she needs to fall in love and get married at the zenith of the relationship to satisfy her craving for attention and thrills. Then, once her life turns into a routine, she's forced to repeat the process for yet another excitement fix.

"She needs that heady excitement of the first rush of love. It is the stress of romance simmering down into an ordinary day-to-day marriage that she apparently doesn't want to cope with. And that is why . . . I believe she cannot stay married," Dr. Brothers wrote.

Some reports about the split said that Elizabeth was tired of living virtually alone out in the country with a workaholic, penny-pinching husband who even threatened to charge her children fifteen cents for each local phone call they made. Friends said she was angered by Warner's insistence that he sell his beautiful, large Georgetown home and move into a two-bedroom condo which didn't have enough closets for her vast wardrobe. Others claimed that Warner was bothered by photos of his wife hanging on the arm of *Little Foxes* producer Zev Bufman at parties and incensed at her outrageous dating (including two weeks alone at her Puerto Vallarta villa) with actor Tony Geary after she made some guest spots on the daytime soap *General Hospital.*

Even though their relationship had obviously cooled to the point where he left a good-luck note rather than accompany his wife to the hospital when she was to have some skin cancer removed, Warner said they had merely drifted apart. Even a year later he said he'd be happy to take her back. By that time, however, Elizabeth had already bought herself a house in Bel Air and was back on the glamorous show-biz social circuit.

Elizabeth turned fifty while in London, and Bufman

threw her an extravagant party. To her delight, Richard Burton called up and asked to be invited, then the two ex-lovers knocked back drinks and discoed in their stocking feet half the night, sparking rumors about a third Burton-Taylor reunion.

Soon afterwards Burton announced his impending matrimony with Sally Hay. In turn, Elizabeth flung herself into the arms of old flame Peter Darmanin, stung by the way Burton had apparently used her to get himself back into the limelight. The only Burton-Taylor reunion was on the stage for their run of the critically disdained *Private Lives,* for which they each received an unheard-of $70,000 a week.

The reality of her flagging career and the loss of yet another husband sent Elizabeth tumbling into a deep depression. Excessive drinking and eating sent her weight soaring up forty pounds and she was soon bulging out of her designer dresses again.

While at a friend's home in Puerto Vallarta, the unhappy woman met a wealthy Mexican lawyer to whom she turned for advice about obtaining a divorce from Warner. Victor Gonzalez Luna provided Elizabeth with more than legal advice—he soon became someone she could lean on, someone she could love, and someone on whom she would once again pin her hopes for a happy life "until death do us part."

Married when he met her, Luna was soon divorced from the mother of his five grown children and busily wooing Elizabeth throughout the fall and winter of 1982.

Despite Luna's attentions, the stress of her divorce and a possible eighth impending marriage proved overwhelming for the actress. At one point she thought she was having a heart attack and was rushed to the hospital in an ambulance, only to find out that nothing was wrong with her. A few months later she collapsed while visiting him in Mexico, and again a screaming siren bore her off to doctors who ascribed her high blood pressure and hyperventilation to stress.

No TV or film roles in which she was the slightest bit interested came her way. Then, in a move which only succeeded in making her feel a hundred times worse, Burton married Sally Hay that July.

Things were crumbling all around her, and Elizabeth coped with her misery in the usual way calculated to grab the most headlines and make her feel the best. In mid-August, while the TV cameras ground away, she waved the sixteen-and-one-half-carat sapphire and diamond ring Luna had presented to her and announced their engagement.

But this time the excitement fix just didn't take. Something was still wrong with her life . . . very wrong. Before long she'd discover exactly what the problem was, but that would involve the hardest lesson she'd ever learn in her life.

"I was at a low in life," Elizabeth admitted in a magazine interview. "I really had nothing of my own to do. I felt very redundant in Washington. I felt unneeded, unnecessary. My children were all grown. And I became terribly fat."

She also admitted she was destroying her body with pills and booze. "I'd been taking at least two sleeping pills every night for thirty-five years. I was hooked on Percodan.

"I'd always taken a lot of medication for pain. I'd

had nineteen major operations, and drugs became a crutch. I wouldn't take them only when I was in pain," she'd added softly.

"I needed oblivion, escape."

Before going to one of the frequent parties she graced with her presence, Elizabeth would attempt to wash away her shyness by downing one or two Percodans with a slug of booze. That combination loosened her tongue and made her feel witty and vivacious. Years later, looking back on that period, Elizabeth realized that the opposite was probably true.

At regular intervals during the evening she'd pop another Percodan, and the drinking never stopped. "I had a hollow leg," she explains. "I could drink anybody under the table and never get drunk. My capacity to consume was terrifying."

Yet she never thought her drinking was a problem and figured she could quit drinking whenever she wanted to. In fact, she had always stopped drinking when staying at health spas, but somehow found herself holding a glass of booze at the next party she would attend.

After a while, however, the booze and pills didn't magically make her the belle of the ball. "I would try to say something, and the thought from my brain wouldn't reach my tongue," she says. "I was stuttering. I was stumbling and it terrified me."

She remembers often coming home after a night of drinking, then popping sleeping pills and Valium to unwind. When she woke up in the middle of the night to go to the bathroom, she was so doped up she'd walk smack into a wall.

In late November she checked into St. John's Hospital in Santa Monica, doubled over from pain, and began having tests for colitis. She kept a bottle of Jack Daniel's sitting on her nightstand, and used it to wash down Demerol and other painkillers. No one in the hospital told her not to mix the alcohol with the medications she was taking.

One day she was pleasantly surprised to see her brother, her sister-in-law, three of her children, and her close friend Roddy McDowall march into her room.

"I was in such a drugged stupor that I thought, 'Oh, how nice, my family are all here to visit.' "

But gradually, she realized something different was about to happen. Howard and Mara had flown in from New Mexico, and one of the kids had been living in New York. Had they really come this far just because of her bowel obstruction?

One by one, the closest people in her life read out loud from letters they'd written to her. Everyone poured out his or her deepest feelings: telling her how much she was loved, how she was the most important person to them. Then they all coldly recited the incidents they had witnessed involving her alcohol and drug abuse.

"Each [was] saying that if I kept on the way I was with drugs, I would die," she recalls.

Elizabeth knew then and there that she'd reached a stage where she needed help desperately. "I realized that my family wouldn't have come unless I'd really reached the bottom." Although surprised by their words, she didn't harbor any anger toward her loved ones—instead, she was flooded with a tremendous feeling of guilt. It was devastating that her very own children had to be the ones to tell her what a mess she had become.

After they had finished reading from their letters, her family told her that they wanted to take her immediately to a treatment program, but she insisted on being left completely alone for a couple of hours.

Liza was especially adamant that her mom come this instant to the car they had waiting, but Elizabeth stood her ground and refused to be pushed around.

She was left to herself. Later, Elizabeth said, "That was the most introspective two hours of my life."

For suddenly she realized that she'd been trying to destroy herself for three and a half decades. What had begun after marrying Nicky Hilton had continued unabated until that moment.

"I became a drunk and a junkie with great determination. And with the same great resolve that got me to that point, I could turn it to work for me," she says today.

So, that very night, December 5, 1983, the fifty-one-year-old actress had her family drive her out to the Betty Ford Center for drug and alcohol rehabilitation on the grounds of the Eisenhower Medical Center in Rancho Mirage, California. She had reached the decision completely on her own . . . she had opted for life.

Once the doors swung shut behind her, Elizabeth's world changed completely. Here was a woman who had never even had to contend with the simple discipline a child learns in school, a woman who was used to indulging her every whim the second it struck her fancy—suddenly subjected to a rigorous, mandatory routine. She wasn't treated as a celebrity, nor was she accorded any of the niceties she deemed her prerogative as a star.

From the moment she signed her name on the admitting papers, she became a plain, everyday person just like everyone else. No special privileges, no favors. She had chosen to "take the cure," and that was fine—but she had to do it the Betty Ford way or not at all.

There were no bars on the windows, no locks on the door. She could "go over the wall" (as the patients jokingly called escaping) simply by calling a cab.

But she didn't. Elizabeth remained in the $130-a-day (currently up to $155) program for seven weeks, three weeks longer than what is considered normal. Instead of having her own luxury suite complete with private rooms for her un-housebroken dogs, she shared a small room with a total stranger and slept in a hard, single bed. Rather than a flock of servants catering to her slightest fantasy, she took out the garbage and washed down a patio. There were no gourmet meals catered by the finest chefs in the world; she ate in the cafeteria with some sixty other patients. Sumptuous gowns by Dior and Valentino were nowhere in sight; her everyday clothes were sweat suits and jeans.

Every day she went to Alcoholics Anonymous–style meetings, group therapy sessions, and had private conversations with a counselor. In group therapy she was fair game just like all the other patients. There was no hiding behind the veneer of beauty, fame, or talent: all her cherished illusions about herself were shattered one after the other.

"After a while, all of your gimmicks and tricks are

stripped away. You're raw, defenseless." But from that position, she found she could build herself anew. Although it was terribly hard, she could no longer hide from the truth that she had become dependent upon alcohol and sleeping pills.

Day by day, she got more in touch with herself—the real self she had never gotten acquainted with before. "It was like peeling an onion—layer by layer," she later told a reporter.

Along with all the other patients, Elizabeth had to keep a journal every night. In it she poured out her pain and loneliness—after all, this was the first time in her life she wasn't surrounded by an adoring entourage.

One of the scariest moments was sitting on the rockhard bed in her room, waiting for the nurse who would help her through detoxification—a woman she imagined to be like Nurse Ratched in *One Flew Over the Cuckoo's Nest.* She had no clothes other than those on her back, nothing to read, no radio—and there hadn't even been a cup of tea awaiting her.

"I was just waiting, and there was no one to explain anything to me. I never felt so lonely or afraid in my life."

The nurse, whom Elizabeth described as a "darling little blond" finally arrived, and the actress let out a big sigh of relief upon discovering that no one was going to scold her. For the first ten days the nurse was with her constantly, and the star found herself opening up and speaking about things she'd never discussed before.

Elizabeth also remembers that it was the first time in her life that no one was trying to exploit her.

Although lonely, Elizabeth wasn't completely without visitors. On Christmas night mom Sara and fiancé Luna ate a turkey dinner with her in the cafeteria. "It was not a happy time," Luna recalls. "They were very strict, no privileges to anybody. At a certain time, we had to leave and no exceptions."

"I've never been more proud of her," loyal Sara gushed about her daughter's treatment. "Elizabeth made the decision all on her own. Thank goodness she's aware of the problem."

At the same time, an embarrassed Luna downplayed the seriousness of his wife-to-be's hospitalization. "I'm surprised that so much has been made of Elizabeth's illness," he said. "This has nothing to do with hard drugs. She merely became dependent on some drugs that she had been using to sleep."

For the patient, however, recovery wasn't quite so simple. Withdrawal was sheer hell. "My heart feels big and pounding," she wrote in her journal. "I can feel the blood rush through my body. I can almost see it, running like red water over the boulders in my pain-filled neck and shoulders, then through my ears and into my pounding head. My eyelids flutter. Oh God, I am so, so tired."

Little by little her strength returned, along with a feeling of serenity she'd never really enjoyed before. She discovered the necessity of living life one day at a time. "It's not like seven weeks there undoes years of drugs and alcohol. You have to re-create what you learned every day," she says. "Staying clean becomes a dedication."

When remaining sober becomes difficult, she finds it enormously helpful to softly repeat the A.A. "Serenity Prayer," and to remember the inviolable pledge she made to herself.

On January 20, 1984, after successfully completing the program, Elizabeth proudly attended a graduation ceremony and wiped away her tears as she was awarded a medallion for her hard work. It is now one of her cherished possessions, something she worked as hard to earn as her two Academy Awards.

In conquering her dependencies, Elizabeth did an incredible thing to aid the fight against drug and alcohol abuse. She was the first celebrity who made it okay to admit openly to having a serious problem, and then to seek the proper help to end that self-destruction.

Although far too many stars—from Marilyn Monroe, Judy Garland, and Janis Joplin, to Errol Flynn, Jim Morrison, and John Belushi—get sucked into the muck of alcohol and the mire of drugs, and lose, Elizabeth fought back—and *won.*

In the following years many would follow her example at the Betty Ford Center. Some celebrities would be successful, but others would sadly fail.

By bravely opening that door for herself, Elizabeth opened it for us all.

"The Elizabeth who went in looked like a tubby person who drank," said one friend. "But she came out looking like a radiant, healthy new woman."

# Chapter Four

*"Like the invisible worm that eats at the heart of the rose, drugs and alcohol are dark, secret lovers that destroy."*—Betty Ford

ON fourteen beautifully landscaped acres of high-priced desert located just eleven miles southeast of Palm Springs, there is a special kind of resort where celebrities and common folks mingle as equals. Unlike the other posh playgrounds in the area, however, the normal party toys our society has deemed completely acceptable and made readily available are strictly *verboten.*

This place is not a glamorous spa where wealthy guests are pampered and catered to with unspeakably wonderful delights for the body and mind. Nor is it a deluxe fat farm where the wealthy go to nibble on carved carrots and swim off a few extra éclair indulgences. It is not another chic tennis or golf clinic where competitive amateurs enroll to perfect their backhands or rid themselves of an unsightly slice.

Although the accommodations in the low-slung modern concrete buildings surrounded by the San Jacinto Mountains are not at all luxurious, the facility currently charges $155 per day, offers very limited recreational facilities, and provides no maid or room service, yet it is 100-percent occupied all year around and has a two- to three-week waiting list.

This is a place where people hope to be dried out by more than just the hot desert air—it is a place where alcoholics and drug addicts of all kinds come to finally end their hellish nightmares of substance abuse.

Welcome to the Betty Ford Center, located at 39000 Bob Hope Drive in posh Rancho Mirage, California. You are entering a very special place which truly understands and—most important—successfully helps people suffering from chemical dependencies.

The mere fact that the center was established in 1982 by the wife of Gerald Ford, the thirty-eighth president of the United States, is enough to make it noteworthy. After all, anything a First Lady does attracts a great deal of attention, and nearly all the presidents' wives have been involved in some sort of philanthropic work or another.

But, when one adds that Betty Ford herself is a recovering substance abuser, and that she remains so active in the center that she actually lectures there once a month, one can quickly see that this is the ultimate chemical-abuse treatment center. No wonder Elizabeth Taylor chose it over programs closer to her home in Bel Air.

In fact, it was after a private conversation with Mrs. Ford, during which she was told, "We are the abused—not really the abusers," that Elizabeth opted to enter the center.

Soon after arriving, Elizabeth realized that the press was hot on her trail, and asked Mrs. Ford if it was wise to come out with a statement about entering the hospital. After all, the former First Lady herself had insisted in a press release that she was merely "chemically dependent," not a drug or alcohol abuser, before entering the Long Beach Naval Hospital to take part in a similar program at the urging of her family in 1978.

After a long discussion with Betty Ford, Elizabeth decided to announce publicly her admittance into the center. Although she was afraid that friends and fans alike might disapprove of her actions, that did not happen. "My friends have been totally supportive, and if anything, they feel relief and pride," she says.

Elizabeth was very lucky that Mrs. Ford in particular and the United States in general had broken open the door to a more enlightened attitude and social acceptance toward controversial matters such as substance abuse, homosexuality, sex without marriage, and divorce. After all, it was not so many years ago when a divorced man such as Ronald Reagan would have been called morally unfit to be the country's chief executive, and when a woman such as Betty Ford, who openly admitted to being a drug addict, would have been shunned socially.

At the beginning of her own treatment, Betty Ford had reached a low point in her life, not unlike the one making Elizabeth miserable. "I walked, I talked, I was polite when you got my attention . . . and I had no particular will to live," Ford told a reporter.

She was terrified to enter the Naval Hospital—of having her narcotic crutches taken from her, of telling total strangers her innermost feelings, of facing up to just how serious her addiction problem had been and the ways she had hurt her loved ones. Because she has been through the treatment program herself, Ford well understands the range of emotions an addict undergoes—the sadness, despair, loneliness and disappointment.

After successfully completing the program, Ford promised to devote her life to helping other addicts—especially women. She feels that women have special addiction problems that are often not recognized in treatment programs.

"A drinking man is macho; a drinking woman is an embarrassment," Ford says softly. Since so many women stay home, they can hide their problems easier and longer. By the time they seek help, women are often in much worse physical and mental shape than male substance abusers.

Other statistics concerning women alcoholics are equally frightening: nine out of ten men walk out on an alcoholic wife, while only one in ten women abandons an alcoholic husband.

"Most facilities dealing with chemical dependency groups are geared to men, and even in coeducational treatment programs, women are more likely to focus on the men and stay locked into their traditional role of nurturing others and putting the needs of others before their own," says one center spokesperson.

For this reason, Ford decided that one wing at the center and a special part of the program would be devoted strictly to women's special problems. One particular problem she was especially familiar with was the all-too-common overmedication of middle- and upper-class women. Doctors will frequently prescribe a pill when the woman should really be getting a completely different type of help, such as psychotherapy.

Together with her former gynecologist, Dr. Joseph Cruse, and the former Ambassador to Belgium (and son of the Firestone Tire and Rubber Company's founder), Leonard K. Firestone, Ford began gathering the $5.8 million needed to build the six-building rehabilitation complex on the grounds of the Eisenhower Medical Center.

The therapy is patterned closely after the one Ford attended at the Naval Hospital, as well as the program offered at one of the country's most respected rehabilitation hospitals—Hazelden in Center City, Minnesota. All these programs are in turn based on the precepts first conceptualized by Alcoholics Anonymous.

When patients walk past the center's thick glass doors and are greeted with a friendly smile and a handshake before signing in, they have already taken the first big step toward their recovery—they have admitted to having a problem.

"Denial is the most important symptom of addiction," Ford insists. "Alcoholics tend to be high achievers and very sensitive—a terribly difficult combination. In their own minds, it's hard for them to believe they are drinking as much as they are."

Added to that denial are the resentment and anger that make substance abusers feel they are different from all the other people who are able to keep their drinking under control.

The center's airy white buildings include one for administration, one reserved for family education, and four comfortable dormitories that sleep twenty people each—all arranged around a central green lawn. Each two- or four-person room opens onto a sunny patio overlooking the desert vistas, the nearby mountains, and the center's flowering pear trees. No one is allowed a private room.

Elizabeth admits that her stay at the center was the first time in her life that she ever shared a room with another woman. Her roommate was a young drug addict, and by the end of her stay the star had taken on a very motherly, protective attitude toward the young woman.

The shared rooms are pleasant but far from opulent. The plain wooden headboards are reminiscent of those in motels, as are the bedside reading lamps. Between the single beds stands a six-drawer dresser, and hanging on the walls are colorful prints. Against one wall are wooden closets that coordinate with the headboards.

Without exception, the patients are required to make their own beds immediately after arising every day at 6:15 A.M. Although some people are shocked to learn that there is no one to do their laundry or make the beds, Ford says that everyone soon learns that "humility is an important aspect of our program" and realizes that he or she is a *part* of the group where no one is of higher status than anyone else.

In addition to keeping one's room clean, patients are assigned to do other chores that are rotated weekly, such as vacuuming or setting the tables. It is the center's belief that a little menial labor is highly therapeutic. The very act of cleaning brings both a feeling of accomplishment plus the sheer joy one gets from living in spotless surroundings. (Never mind that it is also symbolic of cleaning up one's life. . . .)

Elizabeth's first assignments were hosing down the

patio and taking out the garbage. "I got into it," she said in an interview. "I was very proud of that patio. The garbage? I don't know anybody who likes taking out garbage. But it's something that has to be done." Since everyone is pitching in and doing his or her chores for about a half an hour, Elizabeth pointed out that she didn't even think about them after a while.

After making their beds, the patients meet for breakfast, then take a walk around the grounds, enjoying the crisp, clean air and surrounding beauties of nature. The therapeutic chores are next. By nine o'clock, everyone is seated, listening to the morning lecture. An hour later they split up into groups of five and meet in their counselors' offices for therapy. After that comes lunch, then the afternoon lecture, followed by another group meeting. The late afternoon is devoted to exercises—either swimming or aerobics. The 5:15 dinner is followed by a lecture, and the evenings are devoted to reading and writing assignments.

Privileges for patients are few. No phone calls—in or out—are allowed during the first five days, and there is only one phone in each dorm. Newspapers can only be read after 7:00 P.M. and both magazines and books (except the approved ones in the bookstore geared to the patients' treatment) are banned. Only on Saturday and Sunday are a limited number of programs allowed on each dorm's solitary TV, and visitors are prohibited except on Sundays and holidays between 1:00 and 5:00 P.M. Of course, no patient can leave the grounds during the first twenty-eight days at the hospital.

Each patient's luggage is carefully searched upon admission into the center, as no one is allowed to have any type of pills, vitamins, or even grooming products such as perfume, after-shave, or mouthwash. (Some desperate people in the throes of withdrawal have been known to drink them for their alcoholic content.) Patients requiring medication for ailments must pick it up every day at the nurses' station in their dorm.

The writing assignments are harrowing, even for a professional writer. Barnaby Conrad, author of the best-selling novel *Matador* and twenty-one other books, writes in *Time Is All We Have: Four Weeks at the Betty Ford Center* that his counselor Jerry told him many times that the writings in his journal were "unacceptable."

Unaccustomed to receiving negative feedback for his literary efforts, Conrad demanded to know why his work wasn't up to snuff.

"No feelings," he was told. "You've been way out of touch with your feelings for years. Maybe decades. Your feelings, like those of most drunks, have been anesthetized." Jerry then instructed him to redo the assignment.

Topics the patients must examine in writing include: listing twelve consequences of their drinking which occurred during the past two years, ways they can improve how they feel about themselves, and incidents such as "My Most Humiliating Experience."

Conrad dashed off what he considered a "polished, professional account" of the two weeks he spent behind bars on a drunk-driving charge. The group members called his piece "racist," "B.S.," and "showin' off." The writer was even further stunned to have his counselor announce that he was in "deep trouble" because he hadn't turned in his revised assignment or his journal entries.

Each patient is also given nightly reading assignments from the Alcoholics Anonymous book *Twelve Steps and Traditions.*

Towards the end of the patients' treatment, their families are requested to join them for a week-long session devoted to coping with the new person who will soon be returning home, and how not to undermine the recovering addict's good intentions.

Fiancé Victor Luna joined Elizabeth during this week, then remained in Palm Springs an additional week to give her further emotional support.

At some point during the treatment, patients discover for themselves the truth in the AA's words that all people need to "make a decision to turn our will and our lives over to the care of God *as we understand him.*" It is a magical, personal, and intensely spiritual moment.

When that time came to Elizabeth, she knew that God had not forsaken her, and got down on her knees with her young roommate to say thanks.

Betty Ford says that each person turns the corner toward recovery when it is least expected. Hers came "down by the coffee machine kibitzing with two black seamen playing cards. In my everyday life, I would never have met these men, but they and I helped to heal one another.

"We often share tears," Ford adds, "but they are healing tears." So many addicts feel that crying is an emotional weakness that they've numbed their emotions into an icy submission. Once the tears come out, along with the years of pent-up emotions, the abuser is back in control and the healing process which brings a new life can begin.

Although strict and rigorous, the program is also eminently effective. Three-fourths of the center's former patients were recently interviewed for a study, and it was found that eighty-one percent of them had not returned to using drugs and/or alcohol.

The medallion presentation ceremony is held in the living room of the dorm, a room with a lofty vaulted ceiling and an enormous stone fireplace. As the departing patient is handed the half-dollar-sized bronze-colored coin, all weep with sorrow and joy. Sorrow because they will miss a true friend they've grown to know and love in a few short days or weeks, and joy because they know that the person is leaving for a new life filled with health and happiness.

Former patients who find themselves wavering in the sight of temptation often gather the inner strength and courage needed to continue their fights against substance abuse by gazing at the medallion. On its surface is etched the AA prayer: "God grant me the serenity to accept the things I cannot change, the courage to change the things I can, and the wisdom to know the difference."

Ford's medallion is kept in her wallet to remind her that she is a recovering alcoholic who knows where to turn for help should she ever find she needs it.

She remembers, all too well, a time two months into her sobriety when she had to give a party and all the pressures she put herself under came rushing back. Wishing desperately that she could have just one Valium to calm her down, she spotted a pitcher of her husband's martinis. No one was around, no one would ever know if she gulped some of the mixture down.

Fiercely holding onto her self-control, Ford forced herself to think of all the people who had convinced her to seek help. She knew that slipping back would hurt them as much as it would her—and she was able to fight off the temptation.

The road to recovery from substance abuse is long, hard, and never-ending. There will always be a party when an unknowing (or uncaring) host insists that "Just one little glass of wine won't hurt you," or the late night at the office when everyone is tooting up a line of coke to help get the big project done before dawn, or a tense moment when one "needs" a little pill to calm down. Recovering abusers must fight constantly to avoid the things most people never give a second thought to imbibing.

Yes, it's a long, hard road, but the new, wonderful life it brings is well worth all the pain and work. Barnaby Conrad said he felt as though he'd been on a month-long ocean cruise "sharing the many ups and downs and small adventures and intimacies of a voyage, a voyage of discovery."

Elizabeth also felt as if she'd been on such a journey, and the thing she'd discovered was her love for her family and for herself. "I'm enjoying life so much that I want to spend time and energy on me and the people I love, the people around me. I want to live my life," she said.

# Chapter Five

*"I'll be damned if I ever let myself get that heavy again!"*—Elizabeth Taylor

THE Elizabeth who rushed out the doors into the waiting arms of fiancé Victor Luna was a completely different woman from the one who had crept into the Betty Ford Center in the dark of night six weeks before. She felt healthier than she had in years and she was eleven pounds lighter.

The weight she'd lost had mostly been the bloat that alcoholics lug around in their bodies. However, after she stopped drinking, her metabolism changed wildly and she developed an enormous craving for candy and other sweets. Although it is normal for many recovering alcoholics, it nearly turned her into a chocoholic.

One thing she had loved the most about living in Virginia was the food. Her favorite meal is a plate loaded with fried chicken, mashed potatoes smothered in gravy, corn on the cob slathered with several pats of butter, and a mound of lima beans—all followed by something made from chocolate and loaded with calories for dessert.

Down on the farm she wore lavish, flowing caftans

to hide her bulk. Since she never bothered to glance in a mirror, she didn't realize just how obese she'd become. Looking back on the photos from the period, she gazes in the face of a terribly unhappy woman.

Elizabeth feels that Washington, D.C., is home to more unhappy wives than any other place in the world because very few of the women have their own careers or lives. The woman helps her husband to get elected, then he ignores her for the good of the country.

"The senate becomes the wife, the mistress," Elizabeth explains. "That was one lady I couldn't begin to fight. She was too tough."

Whenever she felt sorry for herself, she'd indulge in something fattening. One favorite comfort was chocolate ice cream covered with a thick layer of hot fudge sauce. "Poor Elizabeth. Let's have a little reward, then," she'd tell herself before digging in.

Rather than fight the senate for her husband's attentions, she just gave up and filled the empty spots in her life with piles of rich food. During better times in her life Elizabeth had been obsessed with her looks, but during her years in Washington she looked the other way.

"I let my hair go, I didn't bother with makeup," she says. "I obviously just didn't care."

But despite not caring about her appearance, Elizabeth was not happy when she was fat. Although she pretended she was amused by all the fat jokes circulating about her, deep inside she was terribly hurt by the unkind remarks.*

* The jokes bandied about by Joan Rivers during Elizabeth's fat years would have hurt anyone. "Elizabeth Taylor is the only person who stands in front of a microwave oven and screams, 'Hurry!' " the

She feels that rebellion was part of the reason why she let her weight go up so high. Since elementary school she had been a working actress, pushed into one film after another. However, her weight was one thing she could have control over. "I reached a point in my life where I thought, 'No, damn it! If I want to be fat, I'll bloody well be fat.'"

But she was only hurting herself. She was a grown woman now, no longer under the thumb of either MGM or her domineering mother. And, as a grown woman, she realized she could be as happy as she made up her mind to be.

That philosophy also worked the same way with her weight. She could be as thin as she wanted, for the rest of her life, just by getting into the proper mental set.

"You have to try to get your head at the right place," she explains. "Where you can make it click. Without that inner click, it doesn't matter how many fad diets you go on."

Now that she felt so free and light in her spirit from kicking the booze and pain-killers, Elizabeth felt an

---

blonde comedienne deadpanned. "When I took Elizabeth Taylor to Sea World it was so embarrassing. Shamu the Whale jumps out of the water; she asks if it comes with vegetables!" The jokes went on for months, and seemed to get more and more vicious.

The rift was finally healed when Rivers found she could no longer tease a beautifully slimmed down Elizabeth. "You can't do it when she's thin," Rivers said. "But I am hoping she'll become anorexic, because that will open up a whole new ball game."

The two women met for the first time when they co-hosted a benefit party for the Intercouncil of Abused and Neglected Children in November 1985. Wallis Annenberg, who shared the head table with them, said the former adversaries "really hit it off. They're like new best friends. And why not? They're both very bright. Both warm and gracious."

overwhelming desire to rid herself of the hefty body that was weighing her down, and immediately began to diet.

The true test of her new mental attitude came during times of depression or when she became ill or injured. A miserable, bedridden Elizabeth would stuff herself with malteds and ice cream in a vain attempt to take away her boredom and self-pity.

After such a downturn she soon found herself packing on the weight she'd tried so hard to lose. One time she even gained back half of the total fifty pounds she'd lost. All at once she was hit by a revelation which has enabled her to get slim and stay there: Elizabeth realized that eating fattening foods wasn't making her feel better—it actually made her feel worse!

Losing her self-control made her feel ashamed, and once the pounds started to pile up, she felt that she looked horrid and ugly. That misery created an open season for even more stuffing her face.

"I could see myself blow up and I finally said No. It's ridiculous. I had a long chat with myself in the mirror."

According to Elizabeth, the most important part of any weight-loss program is "self-esteem." People have to love themselves and what they are doing in life. Happy, content people naturally want to be the best they can—and that includes looking good. Once a person gets into this positive frame of mind, any sensible weight-loss program will be effective. However, without entering this proper mind-set, people keep on acting in their old, self-destructive ways of overeating, drinking too much, and so on.

According to Richard Stewart and Barbara Jacobson, authors of *Weight, Sex, and Marriage: A Delicate Balance,* the key to understanding weight loss for women is realizing that there is a reason behind overeating. Diets alone don't work, because they take the backward approach: eat less and your problems will disappear.

Instead of just concentrating on their intakes, overweight women should seek out the gap they are filling in with food. Is it boredom, loneliness, anger at your spouse or children? Once the basic problem is discovered and dealt with, slimness will come by itself.

However, this isn't as easy as it sounds. "It's more socially acceptable to be working on your weight than talking about marital or self-esteem problems," Jacobson says. "No woman is embarrassed with a diet, whereas she's probably not going to say to her best friend, 'My husband's not affectionate enough.'"

Finding the root problems deep inside herself is exactly what Elizabeth had to do. During the next couple of years she forced herself to delve into her lifelong feelings of insecurity, inferiority, and fears of living alone.

The therapy sessions she'd been through at the Betty Ford Center had opened up the doors to all these scary emotions, and she finally entered those rooms to work on the problems she'd always shunted away because the fear of dealing with them had been too great. At long last she could come to grips with her own unique dichotomy of strength and frailty; award-winning talents and insecurity; beauty and inferiority.

After years of deep revelation, Elizabeth found a person inside herself whom she could admire and love. She found a woman who adores children and animals, a woman with a zest for life, a woman of great talent and one well worthy of happiness.

Right after receiving her sobriety medallion, Elizabeth realized she had tentatively stepped onto the road of feeling good about herself. She decided that this would be a perfect time to pamper herself a little while dealing with her weight problem. Soon after checking out of Betty Ford, she checked into the Palm-Aire, a glamorous spa near Ft. Lauderdale, Florida. It was probably the best move she could have made at that point in her life.

For one thing, she'd always stopped drinking whenever she entered a spa in the past, so this was one old pattern she could fall back on that would actually help her. The spa's healthful emphasis on exercise and delicious light meals also gave her more energy and a feeling of well-being she hadn't enjoyed in years.

As the pounds began to melt off, Elizabeth began to develop the weight-loss program—and inner strength —that would enable her to shed a total of forty-five pounds in two months.

Losing weight is never easy, especially for someone who loves to eat as much as Elizabeth. Once her hairdresser, Zak Taylor, saw her gaze longingly into her refrigerator and moan, "Oh, I would love to bite you, and you, and you . . . !"

Like most people fighting the battle of the bulge, she found that she needed motivational boosts to keep her on her diet.

"I read in the paper that someone had a fat picture of me on her refrigerator to keep her from eating," Elizabeth laughingly told an interviewer. "I said to myself, 'Well, if it helps her, it ought to help me.' You ought to see the awful picture I have of myself on the icebox door."

Not drinking calorie-laden alcoholic beverages was another tremendous help in shedding the pounds rapidly.

Elizabeth discovered that if she followed a few simple rules, she lost weight the fastest and was able to keep it off.

She told a reporter that fruits and vegetables were promoted from occasional side dishes into menu mainstays. Red meat was completely cut out; instead, she developed a taste for such low calorie foods as fish and chicken barbecued with lime.

The rich, fattening desserts she used to gorge on are not allowed.

According to a source, for breakfast she would have a serving of oatmeal topped with a few raisins, a sprinkling of nutmeg, and some nonfat milk.

And now she eats slowly, putting her fork down between bites. She always chews all her food thoroughly before swallowing.

"I don't think I ever really chewed before," she said once. "My jaw is finding muscles I never knew I had!"

Elizabeth's regular diet probably averages between 950 and 1,200 calories a day. However, she told an interviewer that she allows herself one day every week when she "pigs out" on whatever she wants.

"Life on a total diet for the rest of one's life would be totally depressing," she explained to a journalist.

The indulgence usually doesn't budge the scale on her daily weigh-in, but if she should gain two pounds, "for the next two days I really have to watch it."

However, she cautioned people wanting to lose

weight that they must maintain their goal for at least a month before allowing themselves a pig-out day. "You can't fiddle around while you're dieting or when you're first maintaining, or you'll blow it," she told the reporter.

Elizabeth found that keeping busy is one of the easiest ways to keep weight off. In fact, when she's working, she never even has to watch her weight.

"It's all part of the regime to discipline. When you're idle you tend to eat more because you have time to think about it," she explained to a journalist. She said that many people who grow bored easily tend to fill the empty spaces by stuffing their faces, rather than filling their minds.

Losing weight isn't generally the problem for most people—what's hard is keeping it off. She said that a person has to truly know herself, deep inside. "Know your own particular traps, your own pitfalls," she advised.

Elizabeth insisted to an interviewer that there is truly no secret formula to losing weight and maintaining it. "It's just common sense. I figure, what the hell, if I can do it, anybody can!"

One of the hardest parts about losing weight was getting herself motivated, and staying motivated. It makes her a little sad that no one—not her children, not her friends, and none of her lovers—ever came up to her when she got so humongous and told her what she was doing to herself.

She would have greatly appreciated some more attention and help from her loved ones during that period, and their words would have woken her up, just as her family was able to when they approached her about her drug and alcohol abuse.

Elizabeth told a reporter that her target was to get her weight down to 125, a goal she has since exceeded. She now weighs a mere 120/121 and boasts a nineteen-inch waist. When she looks in the mirror, she now loves the woman she sees.

Her dress size is now a six—down from her all time high of a fourteen—and her waist is as small as it was when she was shooting *Cat on a Hot Tin Roof.*

Elizabeth has adhered to a program of light exercise to help her stay in shape. According to a source she continued to practice the stretching and toning workout she learned at Palm-Aire, and had a trainer lead her through a routine of water exercises in her pool at home. Although she'd love to horseback-ride more, her bad back keeps her out of the saddle.

People everywhere wonder exactly what Elizabeth, hailed as one of the loveliest women to walk the face of this planet, does to stay so gorgeous.

In an interview with a journalist she has said that her basics of skin care are "soap, lots of fresh water, and a good hand lotion—because you can use it on your body, hands, and face."

What? Mere soap and water for the queen of luxurious excess? She doesn't have a chemist on her staff who whips up a special potion for every new problem wrinkle or patch of dry skin?

"I'm serious," she told the reporter. "Cleansing with soap and lots of water, using your hands—I think that's best."

She said she even goes so far as to use the soaps

provided by the hotels she stays in. Only once did this policy cause a problem.

"I was staying in a hospital, and using the soap I found there to wash my face," she laughingly told the journalist. "My skin began to get all dry and flaky. Then I discovered it was a deodorant soap!"

The regimen that Elizabeth Taylor devised during the difficult years has given the Elizabeth of today the kind of radiance that few women—of any age, of any background—can hope to match. Perhaps her dazzling looks, her luminous face in recent months comes from the intensity of her struggle—both mental and physical—to regain control of her life. "I am certainly a compulsive person," she once told a journalist, "but usually, before I reach the abyss, I start pulling back." Thank goodness for that spirit of self-preservation. For across America and all over the world, millions are rooting for her continued success. And of course, who knows how many women—and men—she has inspired to take charge of their own lives? Elizabeth mesmerizes . . . and motivates!

The Elizabeth of the late 1980s dazzles us the way the Liz of thirty years ago did. Whether she wears the most décolleté dresses or tight leather pants, an Oscar de la Renta or a pair of Calvin Klein jeans, she looks every inch the star.

But Elizabeth once revealed to an interviewer that she has never really considered herself beautiful. In fact, she said, she believes her current glow is a mere reflection of her inner well-being. "I think Nature, God, your spirit, whatever you want to call it, takes over after you're forty and chisels what you look like because it mirrors what's inside." True beauty is deeper than even the most beautiful skin.

And whom does this most beautiful of women consider beautiful? Elizabeth confessed to a journalist that she thinks Bette Davis has "a wonderful face. . . . She's had a stroke and coped bravely with so many things." Katharine Hepburn she said "radiates energy" and she even put Rear Admiral Grace Hopper on her list, saying that she was "totally hypnotized" by an interview that this eighty-year-old scientist gave on television. Whom we admire reveals worlds about what we want to be and what we aim for, and Elizabeth's choices show she looks for spiritual as well as physical beauty in people. Of the younger generation of actresses, Elizabeth chose not the simple beauties, but those who intrigue us by their differentness—Sissy Spacek, Meryl Streep, Kathleen Turner, and Debra Winger. What she admired in these women was what America sees emanating from Elizabeth herself—"radiance."

"I think I have an inner peace which is evolving," she told a reporter recently. "I'm very happy right now. I'm sort of beginning to grow up." And her days at the Betty Ford Center, as well as at Palm-Aire, were instrumental in that change. This amazing new Elizabeth who emerged from the spa caught the entire world by surprise. Could this trim blonde wearing a happy smile, healthful glow, and chic outfits really be the same roly-poly brunette bursting out of her jogging suit everyone had seen in the surreptitious photos taken at the Betty Ford Center?

Luna took one look at this vision of loveliness and whisked her off on a celebratory tour of the Far East.

She was definitely a different woman—mugging for the photographers and inviting them out to dinner instead of screaming four-letter insults at them.

"I plan to be on vacation for the rest of my life," she said at the time.

Hand in hand, the couple took in the sights of Asia, including the tear-jerking atomic bomb memorial in Nagasaki, Japan; the exotic street markets in Bangkok, Thailand; India's famed Taj Mahal; plus many cities and historical sites in China. Two photographers from the States who followed them during their entire Eastern adventure said that Luna and Elizabeth both were relaxed, happy, and very much in love.

Shortly after returning in April, Elizabeth was approached by Bill and Jo LaMond, producers of the TV series *Hotel*. "We heard through mutual friends that Taylor likes *Hotel* and would be interested in doing the show," Bill LaMond said. "So we wrote the script [called "Intimate Strangers"] with her in mind and submitted it to her. She loved it and agreed to play the part."

The cast and crew flew into a tizzy when the word spread that Elizabeth would be in the season's opener. The royal treatment began even before she set foot in the studio—a chauffeur-driven limousine picked her up for work each day and took her back home at night.

"It was like the regal Hollywood of old," said one crew member. "Liz was like a princess in a castle—in this case her 'castle' was a thirty-four-foot, lavishly furnished motor home they assigned to her as a dressing room."

Her salary (estimates ranged from $65,000 up to $100,000) was the most anyone has ever received for a guest appearance on the show, but she worked hard to earn every penny. The demanding shooting schedule required that she be on the set between ten and fourteen hours a day for seven straight days, but she was determined to prove that she could stand up to a rigorous television production schedule.

Delighted that the producers had cast the actor she chose as her co-star—childhood friend Roddy McDowall—Elizabeth joyfully threw herself into the role of Katherine Cole, a retired stage actress who is trying for a comeback. She arrived for work every day right on time, and even though she suffered severe muscle spasms in her neck one day, she refused to halt the production for any reason.

Contrary to her reputation of being a prima donna on the set, Elizabeth made friends with all the show's regular stars, chatting and joking easily with them. "Everyone in the world was warning about the problems we were going to have, but I've seen far lesser stars who were fifty times the problem. Her demands were nothing," said the show's executive producer, Doug Cramer.

One day the script dictated that she be escorted down a hallway by actor Shea Farrell. "After about five or six rehearsals she turned to me and said: 'My God, this looks like we're walking down the aisle together—in which case I'm very well-rehearsed,' " Farrell reports.

Since she was such a good sport, the producers gave her the eleven-piece $25,000-plus wardrobe—designed especially for her trim new body—and all the beautiful costume jewelry she wore on the show.

Elizabeth took the part mostly for the exposure it

created. "The lady doesn't need the money," long-unemployed pal Peter Lawford said wistfully. "I hope she gets her own series. Maybe she'll be looking for a male co-star."

Word quickly got out that she'd been a delight to work with on the *Hotel* segment, and Elizabeth was soon flooded with offers of work. She took her time picking and choosing among them.

But before she had a chance to select her next project, some shocking—and completely unexpected—news shook her to the core. The wonderful, talented man who had often been her foil, her co-star, and had twice been her beloved husband, had just died in Switzerland.

# Chapter Six

*"Life with Elizabeth is like waking up and finding a wonderful new toy on your pillow every morning. You never stop being surprised. I worship her."—Richard Burton*

ELIZABETH TAYLOR and Richard Burton. Liz and Dick. He's been called "the King of Broadway." She's been called "the Red Queen," "the Queen of Diamonds," and "the Queen of Hearts."

Their riveting and ongoing love affair probably received more of the world's attention than even the true royal scandal caused by King Edward VIII's adoration of Wallis Warfield Simpson. That two such powerful personalities should have come together during the filming of an equally thunderous story such as *Cleopatra* is so perfectly fitting as to cause one to wonder just which deity had a hand in setting this fireball rolling.

Yet, this world-shaking love story began inauspiciously enough. Already well ensconced in his reputation as an unquenchable drinker, voracious womanizer, and brilliant Shakespearean actor, the man born as Richard Walter Jenkins was in Hollywood during the summer and fall of 1952 with his wife Sybil to film *My Cousin Rachel*. All the British cinema elite in

Tinsel Town would meet for Sunday brunch at the luxurious home of Stewart Granger and his young wife, Jean Simmons.

It was the Burtons' first visit to such a posh residence, and Richard was trying to drown his nervousness with the help of a few Bloody Marys. A woman seated across the pool in a lounge chair lowered the book she was reading and took off her sunglasses to get a better look at him. He smiled warmly and received a chilly twitch of her lips in return.

Anxious to find out who this "extraordinarily beautiful" woman was, he worked around and was introduced to a pregnant Mrs. Michael Wilding. He was shocked by her language, which he described as "ripe stuff," and also a little surprised by the total disdain with which she treated him. "She's so dark, she probably shaves," he later muttered to a friend.

Elizabeth also remembers that initial encounter: "My first impression was that he was rather full of himself. I seem to remember that he never stopped talking, and I had given him the cold fish eye."

Nine years later, when he left an acclaimed Broadway role in *Camelot* alongside Julie Andrews and they were reacquainted on the set of *Cleopatra*, each was much more aware of who the other was. Elizabeth was more than a little envious of Richard's reputation as a "real" actor—one who had successfully performed Shakespeare on the stage. He in turn was awed by her all-eclipsing stardom, her international fame, and the fact that her $1 million fee for the film was four times greater than his $250,000—the highest salary he'd received to date.

The film's publicist, Jack Brodsky, remembers the

*A* beautiful, slim Elizabeth still attends many parties, but now she only sips sparkling mineral water from her wine glass.

RUSSELL C. TURIAK

*After being confronted by her family about her dependency on pain-killers and alcohol, Elizabeth entered the Betty Ford Center on December 5, 1983. Fiancé Victor Luna's many visits helped her through this lonely and introspective period.*

SCOTT DOWNIE/CELEBRITY PHOTO

AIDS PROJECT LOS ANGELES

*Less than two years later, a dramatically changed Elizabeth presented Betty Ford with the Commitment to Life Award at an AIDS fund-raising dinner. Ford, also a recovered alcoholic, often counseled Elizabeth during her stay at the center, and played an instrumental part in the actress's treatment.*

*Elizabeth says she felt useless and was often terribly depressed during her marriage to Senator John Warner. "I let my hair go, I didn't bother with makeup. I obviously just didn't care," she has said.*

*After successfully completing her treatment at the Betty Ford Center, Elizabeth checked into a spa and lost forty-five pounds. A delighted Victor Luna swept Elizabeth off on a tour of the Orient to celebrate her recovery and svelte new shape. As always, Elizabeth charmed every man in sight—regardless of his height!*

*At first Dennis Stein's booming laugh was like a breath of fresh air sweeping through Elizabeth's life, but she soon grew tired of his jokes. Their whirlwind engagement lasted only six weeks.*

*Many people were surprised at rumors sweeping Hollywood that Elizabeth was ready to take on the role of super-bitch Alexis when Joan Collins was engaged in a contract dispute with the producers of Dynasty. Elizabeth quickly squelched the talk—she had never even considered taking the part.*

*After breaking off her engagement with Stein, Elizabeth threw herself into dating. She and Michael Jackson often went to the racetrack, the movies, and met Mr. and Mrs. Lionel Richie at Mikhail Baryshnikov's performance of* Swan Lake.

*Elizabeth was delighted when she and Burt Reynolds shared the honor of being named "Humanitarian of the Year" by the Starlight Foundation, a charity which grants the wishes of dying children.*

*What a difference eight years makes! Elizabeth and long-time pal Liza Minnelli found that alcohol was definitely no fountain of youth—(below) both women look far more beautiful, healthier, and happier now that they have quit drinking.*

*Elizabeth treasures the warm companionship she found with George Hamilton. An avowed health and fitness freak, Hamilton keeps the lovely star on her toes—and on her diet!*

*D*uring their turbulent fifteen-year relationship, Richard Burton and Elizabeth acted in eleven movies together and shared a passionate love and devastating arguments. His infidelities and uncontrollable drinking finally drove an irreconcilable wedge between them. Although their second divorce occurred eight years before his August 1984 death—and each of them had remarried since then—Elizabeth said she still felt as though she were his widow.

*Elizabeth and Rock Hudson met when he chose her to play the part of his wife in the movie* Giant, *and their close friendship continued until his death from AIDS in October 1985. "I love her like a sister," Hudson once said.*

RON GALELLA

*Escorted by a beaming George Hamilton and sporting the shoulders of a teenager, Elizabeth proudly received the Film Society of Lincoln Center's prestigious tribute to "a significant film artist." (Below:) Her mother, Sara (far left), and Lillian Gish (far right) were also present to share her happiness.*

R. J. CAPAK

*While* Malcolm Forbes wore a traditional Scottish kilt, Elizabeth showed off the plume-and-crown diamond clip she bought herself from the Duchess of Windsor's jewelry collection for $623,000. The occasion was Forbes magazine's extravagant seventieth anniversary party, with a guest list of 1,100, including celebrities such as Jerry Hall (below right). Forbes gave Elizabeth a check for one million dollars, earmarked for AIDS research, and she called him her "million-dollar baby."

*Elizabeth presented the award for Best Director at the 1987 Academy Awards.*

*E*lizabeth's campaign against AIDS has taken her on fund-raising efforts around the world and before a senate subcommittee. She is determined to see an end to the disease within her lifetime.

*The raven-haired star's first venture into sponsoring a commercial product is Elizabeth Taylor's Passion, a $165-an-ounce perfume. She chose the name because it best reflects her philosophy and lifestyle. "I have a passion for everything I do," she smiles.*

*S*he's acted in nearly sixty films, married six men, raised four children, suffered through unbelievable tragedies and death-defying illnesses, been grossly fat and dependent on pain-killers and alcohol. Yet somehow, Elizabeth survives the trials thrown in her path and triumphs—her charm and grace intact. She is truly better and more beautiful than ever.

greedy look that came into Burton's eyes when he saw the deferential way with which Elizabeth was being treated. " 'They don't want me,' he said, 'they just want Elizabeth Taylor.' I had the sense that he was struck, at that moment, by the glamour of her stardom, the kind he would have wanted for himself," Brodsky said.

After meeting director Joe Mankiewicz and the rest of the cast, Burton sidled up to Elizabeth and gave her his standard opening pitch that had proved successful in getting dozens of other leading (and countless lesser) ladies into his bed: "Has anyone ever told you that you're a very pretty girl?"

"I said to myself, *Oy gevalt,* here's the great lover, the great wit, the great intellectual of Wales, and he comes out with a line like that," Elizabeth recalls. "I couldn't wait to get back to the dressing room and tell all the other girls."

By the next day, however, things had already shifted. Elizabeth remembers a terribly hung over Burton arriving for rehearsal "quivering from head to foot." She had to steady his hand to help him down a cup of coffee, and his vulnerability made her want to put her arms around him. "When he blew his first line —this great actor—my heart just went out to him."

Much to the chagrin of Eddie Fisher, Elizabeth became a regular at the booze-filled parties in Burton's dressing room. When Fisher would harangue her about drinking too much and try to get her home early, Burton would engage the singer in conversation while deftly exchanging his full wineglass for her empty one. "I absolutely adore this man," she thought.

Gradually Fisher caught wind of the burgeoning romance and tried to leave for Switzerland, but Elizabeth insisted that he stay to aid her adoption of Maria. Then came the night when the three of them were drinking brandy heavily and Burton asked her in front of her husband "Who do you love?" "You," she replied. "That's the right answer," Richard said, "but it wasn't quick enough." Elizabeth then became hysterical and left the villa. Burton, however, stayed, alternately abusing and charmingly apologizing to Fisher.

Humiliated, Fisher ran to New York and convened a press conference to prove that his relationship to Elizabeth was still stable. Calling her in Rome, Fisher demanded that she tell reporters that there was no foundation to the rumors. "I can't say that because it's not true," his wife said. "There is a foundation to the story." A furious Fisher spat out, "Thanks a lot," and they never lived together again.

By the end of the tumultuous filming of *Cleopatra,* all the overtime and extras had boosted Burton's salary to $750,000. He spent $150,000 of it on an emerald brooch Elizabeth desired from Bulgari and $37,500 on a bauble for Sybil. Despite the lavish present, Elizabeth wrote him a letter saying they were destroying too many lives. She stayed away from him during the last few days of the filming, then she retired to her chalet in Gstaad while he went to his home in Céligny.

For two months they didn't see each other until Burton finally called and asked her to lunch. She had her parents drive her to the restaurant and Burton didn't notice her at first in the backseat of their car. The top of his car was down, and Elizabeth caught her breath at the sight of his bright blue eyes, tan skin, and shiny short hair.

That day they just had lunch and talked, but in the ensuing weeks lunch was followed with more private delights. Elizabeth decided "I would be there whenever Richard wanted to call me." Although it wasn't a "very satisfying" role, it was "better than nothing." At the same time Burton said he was "maddened with guilt."

After they finished some additional *Cleopatra* scenes in Paris, Elizabeth wanted to be with Burton, and jokingly asked to be in his next film *The VIP's*. The producers loved the idea. Later she followed him to London where he made *Becket,* and she bought him a quarter-of-a-million-dollar Van Gogh for his suite at the Dorchester. Next they took Liza Todd with them to Puerto Vallarta, Mexico, where Burton was starring in *The Night of the Iguana.*

After that she convinced him to take on every actor's dream role—Hamlet. When in Toronto for rehearsals, they sneaked off to Montreal and got married in the bridal suite of the Ritz Carlton Hotel by an English Unitarian minister, the only person found willing to perform the ceremony. "It was like coming home—a golden warmth," Elizabeth remembers.

A drunk Burton was shouting, "Isn't that fat little tart here yet? She'll be late for the last bloody judgment!" by the time Elizabeth showed up an hour late. Wearing a gorgeous yellow chiffon gown, her head piled high with Italian hairpieces entwined with hyacinths and yellow ribbons, she told the press, "I'm so happy you can't believe it. This marriage will last forever."

Although they'd both hoped that the public would calm down once they made their relationship legal, their wedding only seemed to fan the public's flames of desire to glimpse the famous couple. Every place they went they were mobbed, tugged at, and applauded. Thousands of people stood by the stage door at the Lunt-Fontanne Theater every night Burton performed Hamlet, shrieking, "I saw them, I saw them" after catching a glimpse of the couple.

Elizabeth attended forty of the performances, and never wore the same outfit twice. People who used to ignore them now came up to give Burton a congratulatory pat on the shoulder and his wife a buss on the cheek. Burton's *Hamlet* broke records for the longest run of that play on Broadway.

The couple went on to make a string of highly successful movies together: *The Sandpiper, Who's Afraid of Virginia Woolf?,* and *The Taming of the Shrew.* Even the ones which weren't that good still made millions just on the strength of the stars. And the ones which were good were excellent.

With its raw sexuality and harsh language, *Virginia Woolf* changed the state of the cinema forever. Burton lovingly called it Elizabeth's *Hamlet.* In addition to her one million dollars and percentage of the gross, she was given approval of both the director and her co-star. For the former she chose a "genius" who'd never directed a movie before—Mike Nichols. For the latter she wanted a man whom producer Ernest Lehman felt was too powerful, too virile, too impressive—her husband. She got her way and her Oscar. Burton got his price: $750,000.

The filming was such an intense experience for both

of them that each suffered a sense of loss after it was done. Many have said it was the highlight of their eleven films together.

Soon Burton was also earning the fabled one million dollars per film, and the couple began spending money with abandon. A 120-foot yacht was purchased for $200,000 and renamed the *Kalizma* in honor of their daughters: Kate (Burton), Liza, and Maria.* A quarter of a million was spent refurbishing the ship. The furnishings included a rosewood Regency sofa, Louis XVI chairs covered with yellow silk, dining space for twelve, and two Chippendale mirrors. They spent $150,000 a year to maintain it.

Of course, it was a small price to pay to have a homey place their dogs could reside in rather than having to endure a six-month quarantine during the Burtons' frequent visits to the British Isles. (Before the *Kalizma* was completed, they spent $21,600 a month to charter a yacht for the puppies.)

Maintaining their life-style cost about one million dollars a year, but their taxes were negligible because both were residents of Switzerland. To keep the gleam bright in his bride's eye, he purchased the thirty-three-carat Krupp diamond for $305,000, a $50,000 yellow Indian diamond, the inch-long, inch-thick sixty-carat Cartier-Burton diamond for an undisclosed amount over one million dollars, plus dozens of lesser jewels. They bought a home in Puerto Vallarta and a second one across the street for Burton's study, and con-

---

* The name neglects to include poor little Jessica, Burton's second daughter from Sybil, who was born severely retarded and has been institutionalized all her life.

nected the two with an arching path similar to the
Bridge of Sighs in Venice.

Of course they were now flying most places in their
private jet. Their entourage generally included a hairdresser, a nurse for Maria (now adopted by the Burtons, who required constant medical attention
because of the rigorous operations she underwent to
correct deformities in her hip), Elizabeth's secretary, a
secretary for her secretary, a chauffeur, Richard's
dresser—Bob Wilson—and his wife Sally, Richard's
makeup man, a governess, a tutor, the four children,
dogs, cats, and 156 suitcases.

In 1972, their extravagant three-day celebration at
the Budapest Inter-Continental Hotel of Elizabeth's
fortieth birthday so disturbed the sensitivities of lesser
people around the globe that Burton ended up donat-
ing an equivalent of what he'd spent on the party to
UNICEF's children's fund—$45,000.

By this time their marital problems had begun in
earnest. Despite all his hard work, obvious talents, and
seven nominations, Burton was never awarded an Oscar. Being overshadowed by his wife's career couldn't
have been easy for a man as macho as he. In fact, early
in his career he was considered box-office poison—his
highly dramatic voice and carriage just didn't translate
well to films until Elizabeth showed him how to modify
his abilities for the screen.

Both of them also drank to excess—far, far too
often. "Elizabeth seemed to drink probably as much as
he did, but she wasn't nearly as much affected by it, so
far as one could see. She was stronger than Richard in
every way," remembers Edward Dmytryk, who directed Burton in *Bluebeard*.

Burton went through periods when he'd cut back to only one martini on Sundays, or only a glass of red wine with dinner. Once he swore off alcohol for three months just to prove to Elizabeth that he could.

A sensitive, insightful, and extremely intelligent man, Burton's biggest weakness was his love for distilled and fermented spirits. "I have to think hard to name an interesting man who didn't drink," he often said, and it wasn't until the last year of his life that he openly admitted to being an alcoholic. His capacity to consume was amazing—when he fell off the wagon, it was into three or four bottles of vodka a day.

Perhaps it was the bottle that ultimately destroyed their love. Elizabeth remembers times when he was abusive in his drunkenness, lashing out at her with harsh words and violent fists. Maybe it was Burton's insatiable lust which finally rent them asunder—toward the end, he began a series of what he termed "cathartic infidelities."

On June 26, 1974, a miserable Elizabeth shielded her eyes with dark glasses and told a judge that their life together had become intolerable and their differences were irreconcilable.

Burton, meanwhile, said he felt ten years younger, and "I intend to roam the globe searching for ravishing creatures." The first he encountered was Princess Elizabeth of Yugoslavia. After he pressed her to marry him for three weeks she gave in, only to call it off a short time later after seeing photos of him strolling arm-in-arm through the streets of Céligny with black model Jeanne Bell. She was also livid at his inability to abstain from drinking.

Elizabeth and Richard kept in close touch by phone,

even though she was by now dating Henry Wynberg, used-car salesman and lover *extraordinaire*. When she returned from filming *The Blue Bird* in Leningrad, she and Burton got together, ostensibly to discuss business. Serious dysentery during her time in the U.S.S.R. had caused Elizabeth to lose a great deal of weight, and she looked ravishing. Richard wanted to get back together. Elizabeth agreed—only if he would stop drinking completely.

Both had endured months of torture apart and went around telling the world how delighted they were to be back in each other's arms. In the fall of 1975 they traveled to Israel and Africa. In October they were married for the second time by a district commissioner from the Tswana tribe alongside the muddy, hippopotamus-filled Zambesi River in Botswana. Elizabeth's green dress was trimmed with lace and guinea-fowl feathers.

Their bodyguard Brian Haynes "didn't think their second marriage would last ten minutes. The Burtons had a real love-hate relationship," he said.

That Christmas in Switzerland, Burton spotted a beautiful blond woman skiing and demanded that she be brought up to the house. Elizabeth knew right away that Susan Hunt wasn't going to be just another affair, and filed for her second divorce from Burton a few months later.

Burton spent his remaining years working hard at one project after another. Despite the best intentions of his new wife, she couldn't get him to quit drinking, either. Susan and Burton announced their separation in February 1982, two months after Elizabeth told the world she would no longer answer to Mrs. Warner.

Rumors of a third Liz-and-Dick show began circulating after the two famous lovers reunited at Elizabeth's fiftieth birthday. A couple of days later, she joined him on the stage during his benefit narration of *Under Milk Wood* to tell him "I love you" in Welsh.

Yet, a short time later Burton's eye was caught by Sally Hay, a thirty-four-year-old BBC production assistant working with him in Europe on *Wagner*. They lived together for a year before marrying in July 1983.

The day before he died at age fifty-eight from a cerebral hemorrhage, Burton met with actor John Hurt at his Céligny home. The older man confided that he had earned nearly thirty-six million dollars in straight fees from his films, and though the members of his family were all provided for, he wondered how so much money had dripped through his fingers.*

As Hurt was leaving, Burton lowered his voice to prevent Sally from hearing and said, "*She* still fascinates, you know." Of course, the "she" was Elizabeth. Elizabeth thought her life would fall apart when Burton died. Even if they never got formally back together, they were still completely bound together by their enormous love for each other. Burton's death on August 5, 1984, came a mere six months after her release from the Betty Ford Center, and many friends feared that the shattering news would cause her to fall off the wagon.

But Elizabeth showed an inner strength few knew

---

* Much of it, of course, had maintained the ostentatious Liz-and-Dick days, but a great deal also went to various charities and to support his twelve brothers and sisters. Despite the estimated eighty million dollars he spent, Burton still left an estate valued at close to four million dollars.

she possessed, which enabled her to withstand some of the harshest and cruelest days of her life. She was staying at the San Francisco home of friends when the first call concerning Burton's death came. Thinking it was some kind of a cruel practical joke, she tossed it off. But the calls kept coming, and a white-faced Elizabeth soon began sobbing as she was forced to accept reality. "Even though Richard and I aren't married anymore, I feel like his widow," she cried.

Burton's real widow didn't waste any time setting that matter straight. Right away, she called Elizabeth and asked her not to come to Burton's burial in Céligny because the star's appearance would eclipse the simple memorial service.

Elizabeth was shocked. She and Burton's third wife had not gotten along because Susan had tried to rid her husband's life of everything which even remotely connected him with Elizabeth. But the star had thought things were different with Sally.

Even Sally admitted that Elizabeth had gone out of her way to make her feel comfortable when they first met. "I was very, very nervous indeed about meeting the beautiful Elizabeth Taylor," Sally said. "But I think she realized that. After about an hour, she put her arm around me and said, 'It's okay.' "

The new Mrs. Burton was a wonderful cook, and she often invited the woman she referred to as "E.T." to dinner in London. Smiling Burtons were photographed alongside Elizabeth and Luna, each lady proudly showing off her shiny new engagement ring. During the Los Angeles run of *Private Lives*, Sally and Richard stayed in a room Elizabeth had fixed up especially for them in her home.

Deeply saddened after Sally's phone call, Elizabeth stayed away from Burton's August 9 burial. Graham Jenkins, one of the deceased's brothers, also warned her off. "I told her that it was not right for her to come, there was too much fuss," he said. "It was inappropriate, pure and simple."

When she did show up a few days later, her companions asked the photographers to please leave her in peace at Burton's grave. All their arguments and pleas were in vain— there was even footage on the news that night of her standing at the foot of his grave and arguing with the photographers.

Members of Burton's family begged Sally to reconsider banning Elizabeth from his service in his hometown of Pontrhydyfen, but the grief-stricken widow told the star over the phone: "Don't come. If you turn up, I will walk out."

Later Sally was quoted as saying she was hurting from "not just the loss, but the publicity and the way people are trying to cash in—to hog the spotlight which should be on Richard.

"There is one person in particular who has tried to make capital out of every step this week. But I finally told her to go away—to get lost."

Elizabeth was permitted to attend the service in London held at St. Martin's-in-the-Fields. She arrived uncharacteristically early and was seated in the front row next to Burton's eldest sister. Sally arrived on time—but much later—and was given an aisle seat farther back. Bad feelings grew deeper when Elizabeth invited members of the Jenkins clan and close friends of the actor to lavish receptions both before and after the ceremony. Susan Hunt was also at the service, but

97

Sybil—now married to rock singer Jordan Christopher and happily living in California—stayed away.

A few days later, Elizabeth's chauffeur-driven Mercedes arrived at the modest row houses in Pontrhydyfen where surviving members of Burton's large family still live. She stayed overnight with his sister Hilda Owen. Still grieving over Burton, his relatives were relieved to hear Elizabeth's pledge.

"She still wants to keep her part of the bond and be buried in Pontrhydyfen," Owen said.

During their marriage, Elizabeth and Burton had purchased adjoining grave sites in Pontrhydyfen—vowing to be buried side by side, but Sally made sure that the actor's final resting place was in the Céligny churchyard. Some said it was done specifically to defy his former wife's plan to be by his side throughout eternity. Others said it was simply for inheritance-tax purposes—Britain recognizes the place where a person retires and is buried as the final place of residence and bases the tax rate upon that location.

Before leaving, Elizabeth asked if she could have an oil painting of the cottage Burton was born in, painted by his brother Verdun Jenkins. "We are delighted that she should have it," Owen said. "It was marvelous to have all the family together again, and she was very pleased to be back with us."

A few months later, sparks flew again when Sally wandered over to her husband's grave on Christmas morning and found it covered with a blanket of cream and red roses—courtesy of Elizabeth. Upon learning that several grave sites in the churchyard were for sale, she immediately purchased the one next to Burton to prevent Elizabeth from taking such an action. She then designed a large, double headstone that straddles both graves and had it installed a year later.

Sally had a hard time containing her bitterness over Burton's funeral. Two and a half years later she said, "I feel hurt because Richard's family and Elizabeth made no acknowledgment of my pain. They seemed to be saying, 'She's young, she'll get over it.'

"Everybody was saving their sympathy for Elizabeth. They kept saying, 'Poor Elizabeth.' This really hurt."

Friends of the award-winning actress feel that she will never get over the snub of being asked to stay away from Burton's funeral. She told them that the experience was "the worst in my entire life; worse even than Mike Todd's funeral!"

The thirteen years Elizabeth and Burton spent together (eleven of them in wedlock) was considered by many to have been her only "real" marriage. Elizabeth may have loved Mike Todd more, or differently, but their marriage ended tragically before the honeymoon period had ended. She and Burton had the shared experiences a husband and wife need for a deep, lasting relationship.

The shock of his death caused her to once again reevaluate her life and what she was doing. She decided never to do another play and also decided to break her engagement with Victor Luna.

Although the breakup was announced in the end of August, Elizabeth's publicist Chen Sam said the couple had parted amicably a couple of months before. Some friends hinted that Luna just wasn't rich enough to keep up with Elizabeth's needs, while others said he was a hardworking lawyer who wanted to live a simple life in Guadalajara and couldn't handle the jet-set pace.

"Those were very special times," is how a heart-broken Luna recalled the months spent in Elizabeth's company.

"I'm beginning to learn that happiness can only come from within myself," said Elizabeth.

# Chapter Seven

*"Let's just say I almost made a mistake . . .
but I didn't."—Elizabeth Taylor*

STILL grieving about Richard Burton's death and saddened by her breakup with Victor Luna, Elizabeth avoided both the bottle she could have upended, the sleeping pills she might have popped, and the food she could have gorged upon. Instead, she fell back on her two tried-and-true remedies for overcoming life's losses. First of all, she threw herself back into work.

For her next project, Elizabeth chose the part of Louella Parsons in the TV movie *Malice in Wonderland.* Jane Alexander co-starred as Hedda Hopper.

"I read the script, and I loved it," she said, adding that she was ready for it because doing "eight shows a week (in the theater) is too taxing." Elizabeth also said that having lost weight gave her added courage to take on the part, but kidded, "I should have been playing her a year ago when I was fat and frumpy—like she was."

Given her choice of the two roles, Elizabeth picked Parsons because, "I think Louella was very single-minded and dedicated to her nastiness.

"I had a score to settle with Hedda. When I confided in her as a friend, she blabbed the whole story in her column about my romance with Eddie Fisher. She even made up quotes I had never said or even thought, such as, 'What do you expect me to do, sleep alone?'"

Her vast firsthand experiences dealing with the queens of gossip lent a touch of realism to the role. But when Elizabeth decided to add even more realism, the producers balked.

"She asked for a meeting in her trailer her first day on the set," said producer Jay Benson. "All she told us was that she had a surprise for us. Louella's teeth looked—there's no other way to put it—like a row of Chiclets, and she talked with a slight lisp.

"Elizabeth had gone to a dentist and had a row of caps made that duplicated the look. We considered them, but decided they wouldn't work—the row of Chiclets was just too distracting."

It was decided that the star would remain glamorous, and one way to accomplish that was by adorning her sleek new body with a dazzling wardrobe. And the only designer she wanted to create these spectacular peacock feathers was Nolan Miller, who had designed the duds she wore on *Hotel.*

"I really didn't have time to take on another picture," Miller said, citing his demanding commitment to designing the clothes worn by Linda Evans and Joan Collins on *Dynasty.* But when Elizabeth begged him to create eighteen special fashions just for her, he couldn't say no.

Miller decided on tapered, crisply cut styles. "She's so thin," he gushed. "We didn't want to cover her up with anything baggy, so we kept her clothes simple.

She's a size six with a twenty-four-inch waist, a perfect figure for the clothes of the thirties."

He decided against using the shoulder pads that were so popular on *Dynasty* at the time. "They [Evans and Collins] think it makes their waists look smaller," he explained, adding that Elizabeth's costumes contain almost no padding. "We didn't want to pad her. She's playing a journalist, not someone who looks like she's about to attend a costume party."

For the most part, she adored Miller's costumes, taking home many dresses and *all* the lingerie he had fashioned. Elizabeth did all the fittings herself, and other than requesting a lower neckline in one costume and a tighter waist in another, she never told the designer how to do his job.

The only time she disagreed with his taste was when he draped an antique fur stole around her shoulders—one where the heads of the animals were still attached. "These things were dead even before *I* was born," she sniffed. A new wrap was quickly created.

Elizabeth's behavior on the *Malice* set wasn't quite as exemplary as during the *Hotel* filming. Co-star John Pleshette said the star was "great—when she was there."

Her late arrivals were "less a matter of being unprofessional than that this is what she's been like all the time—the star. It's like she doesn't want to let the public down, and she considers the cast and crew part of the public," he added.

All in all, her tardiness wasn't too terrible—the filming was completed only one day behind schedule. And, many in the cast felt honored to be working with such a great star.

Actress Leslie Ackerman, who played Parsons' daughter Harriet, said working with Elizabeth was even more enjoyable because the older woman stuck so rigidly to her diet.

"It's not like I worked with some humongous actress who said, 'Bring on the chocolate souffles,'" Ackerman joked. "They'd bring us croissants, and she'd say, 'No, bring us fruit.' It was like a dream shoot that way."

A constant dieter herself, Ackerman said she normally has to wait a long time to get low-calorie goodies when on a set. But, "When Elizabeth Taylor asks, three seconds go by and there's a plethora of grapes, apples, and tangerines. . . .I think one time she got in the car with me and confessed that she ate a chocolate bar."

Elizabeth's fee for the twenty-day shoot was nearly $500,000 and, of course, she assumed that most of her wardrobe would also be given to her.

When speaking to Ackerman one day on the set, Elizabeth noted that the other woman had been wearing a certain parka continuously. "It's become your trademark," Elizabeth said. "Why don't you ask the producers to give it to you?"

Ackerman laughed and told the star that she already owned the parka, then inquired if Elizabeth was going to ask for the fur coat she was wearing.

"Of course, darling," was the reply.

"But why?" Ackerman insisted. "You must have twenty fur coats already."

"No, darling," the star purred. "Only about twelve."

Although absorbed in her role of the gossip queen,

Elizabeth still felt something was missing from her life. She quickly dove into her second surefire method to fight depression—she got engaged again.

Not long after she parted from Victor Luna, Elizabeth was seen dating Carl Bernstein (whose claim to fame was *All The President's Men*, as well as other writings about Watergate, and a major role in *Heartburn*, a roman à clef by his ex-wife Nora Ephron). Soon after that, she was introduced to a dashing man-about-the-world—Dennis Stein. With his broad shoulders, salt-and-pepper hair, and booming laugh, Stein was like a breath of fresh air sweeping into her life and cleaning away the cobwebs of unhappiness.

Barbara Sinatra arranged for them both to be present at a pre-Thanksgiving dinner party in the Sinatras' Palm Springs home, and all the other guests could see the immediate chemistry between them.

"I was talking to Elizabeth the next day," said close friend Nolan Miller, "and she said she had met the best-looking man the night before. Then she laughed and said, 'He's even an *available* man.'"

By the end of November, a broadly smiling Elizabeth was seen hanging onto Stein's arm at Spago, Chasen's, and other chic Los Angeles restaurants. One night she donned a spiky yellow wig, and they showed up at a Michael Jackson concert.

Stein was determined that no black moods should tarnish his beautiful star. Joining her constant diet, he managed to shed twenty pounds in the process. Neither a drinker nor an indulger in pills, he helped her to remain far away from both substances. Most important, he kept her extremely happy.

"Meeting Dennis was like being hit with an atomic

bomb," Elizabeth told a close friend. "Within seconds, he had me laughing. It was an immediate attraction for me."

Although his humor had Elizabeth doubled over with laughter, other acquaintances thought his jokes were a bit dry. Columnist Suzy Knickerbocker relates a time when Stein wanted to give her some jewelry. " 'Want a diamond pin?' he said to me once. 'Why not?' I said. Whereupon he presented me with a safety pin with a dime glued to it. Dime-on-pin, get it?"

Another time, New York restaurateur Elaine Kaufman told him she was on a diet, so he sent her a film reel made from three-and-one-half pounds of chocolate.

Pat Seaton Lawford, the wife of Elizabeth's longtime pal Peter, said, "No one is too sure what the real Dennis Stein is like, because he's always joking."

In addition to a well-known sense of humor, Stein had numerous detractors who referred to him as "Dennis the Menace." A divorced man of fifty-two, he had been seen previously with Joan Collins and three Miss Americas hanging on his arm—all on separate occasions, of course. Some detractors have called him "a fake," "a creep," and "a guy Sinatra uses to take Barbara around when Frank is too busy."

Working as a consultant for Technicolor, Stein was a Brooklyn boy who made a fortune selling designer jeans. Some insiders said the rich and famous only kept him around for his connections in the rag trade—he could get top designer gowns at a fraction of their retail price.

Stein scoffed at the tongue-waggers and proclaimed his happiness. "I have to constantly pinch myself that

I'm really with Elizabeth Taylor," he told a friend. "She's the most beautiful woman I've ever seen. She's the most glamorous. And right now, I feel like the luckiest man alive."

Elizabeth was also walking on clouds, and all her friends could do was cross their fingers that she wouldn't fall through.

On December 11, after only four weeks of dating, Elizabeth stunned the world by accepting a $100,000 twenty-carat oval sapphire engagement ring mounted in platinum with two diamonds on either side. He also gave her a couple of little engagement presents: a forty-carat amethyst stone surrounded by diamonds on an eighteen-karat gold chain he'd picked up for $20,000, and a $6,700 watch with a violet mother-of-pearl face.

The day before Stein popped the question, Elizabeth called Luna to spare him the pain of first hearing the news through the media. A heartbroken Luna said he still deeply loved the movie queen, but apparently a marriage between them wasn't meant to be. Calling her "a very special woman" and wishing her "nothing but happiness," Luna added that it was also "the saddest day of my life."

Elizabeth ran around like crazy telling all her children of the impending plans for wedding number eight. "I'm so happy," she told them. "Please be happy for me!"

Then she called her friends—wanting to shout the good news from the rooftops. "He's the only man I've met in years who measures up to Richard and Mike. I've been searching for a man who has the strength, the magnetism, the sheer force of personality and sexiness that Richard and Mike had—and I never found him until I met Dennis," she confided to one crony.

Many of the actress's close friends couldn't help wondering if she was rebounding a little too quickly after Burton's sudden death and her split from Luna, but they all knew the reason why. "Elizabeth doesn't like the single life," one buddy murmured, "and she's the first to admit it. She needs a man in her life."

Ecstatic that her personal life was again blissful, Elizabeth decided to do what she could to aid a friend who wasn't having her good luck. Knowing that Peter Lawford was desperate for work, she arranged for him to play the part of an agent in *Malice in Wonderland*.

An alcoholic for decades, Lawford was terribly ill and in straitened circumstances. What hurt the most was that he had been abandoned by nearly all of his old friends in Hollywood. He called, begged, and pleaded with people to give him just one more chance to act, but all turned a deaf ear.

After her first two weeks in the Betty Ford Center, Elizabeth had called Lawford to join her. He needed to get off the booze that was killing him before he could even dream about making a comeback. Elizabeth spoke so glowingly about the wonders the Center was working on her that Lawford agreed to give it a try. Delighted that her close friend was finally seeking the help he so desperately needed, she generously paid his entire bill—nearly $7,000.

Although Lawford stuck with the program and left in February, some friends said that he continued to drink afterwards. He claimed that he was off booze permanently, but no one in Hollywood would give him a chance to prove himself.

"I haven't been very good to myself," he admitted, his hands shaking uncontrollably. "I have no money, no career. Only a few friends, like Liz Taylor, have stood by me—and that's more than I deserve. The only thing I have left in my life is my wife Patricia, and I've made her life terribly, terribly hard, too."

When he heard that Elizabeth had gotten him work, a grateful Lawford, sixty-one, left his bed in the Cedars-Sinai Medical Center, where he had been admitted just four days before for treatment on his weakened kidneys. "I've never missed a performance, and I'm not going to now," he told his wife.

"Damnit, Liz got me this role when no one else in Hollywood would touch me, and I'm going to prove that I'm a damn professional—and that I can handle it."

A messenger brought his script to the hospital and he studied his lines in bed.

Disregarding his doctor's dire warnings that his liver and kidneys were ruined from a lifetime of hard drinking and that he shouldn't leave the hospital for any reason, Lawford proudly walked out of Cedars-Sinai and got to the set on time, anxious to do his best in the small part. Makeup artists had to work hard to bring a natural glow to his skin, which was terribly yellowed from liver failure.

When the director called out the word "Action!" Lawford froze. The words just wouldn't come.

Nearby, Elizabeth was seen twisting her handkerchief. She had tears in her eyes and she was mumbling a prayer for him under her breath.

Again and again, the director tried to coax the few lines from the formerly polished and debonair actor.

Watching his struggle caused the tears to stream down Elizabeth's cheeks.

Slowly, in the middle of a take, Lawford sank to his knees. He was immediately rushed to the hospital and placed in intensive care. It was December 14, 1984.

Elizabeth visited him often, spending hours at the bedside of her comatose friend, even delaying a European trip she'd planned with Stein. It became clear that Lawford wouldn't make it. Elizabeth told Lawford's wife not to worry about the funeral expenses, and promised to pay for her friend's last tribute. On Christmas Eve, with Patricia beside him, Lawford suffered a cardiac arrest and died.

The same night, a fur-and-diamond-bedecked Elizabeth had just arrived at her chalet in Gstaad accompanied by her new beau. She was terribly saddened by the loss of her friend, but there was no way she could help Lawford now. She cabled her sincere sorrow to Patricia.

Together, Elizabeth and Stein enjoyed a glamorous and carefree Christmas. She had just trimmed down from 118 to a remarkable 111 pounds in ten days by exercising and nibbling on melon slices and lettuce leaves. To celebrate her dedication, Stein treated her to a shopping spree—at Valentino's boutique—which included two $5,000 dresses, nearly $2,000 in other clothing, and a $40,000 black mink coat.

Highlights of their stay in Switzerland included lavish parties studded with stars such as John Travolta, Olivia Newton-John, Ursula Andress, and Victoria Principal. Although friends all around were tossing back glasses of her formerly favorite beverage—champagne—Elizabeth stuck to her vows and toasted them back with mineral water or plain orange juice. She stubbornly showed her resolve by passing up tables groaning under a roast suckling pig, dishes of caviar, lobster, roast goose, and platter after platter of scrumptious desserts at a New Year's party held at the Palace Hotel. Elizabeth ordered a small salad and cheerfully drank in the New Year with Perrier water.

Stein was so proud of his trim darling's willpower that he bought her a $120,000 solid-gold necklace crowned with three heart-shaped rubies and studded with diamonds. His other presents to her included three designer watches ($5,000 each) and a ruby and rock crystal necklace with matching earrings ($15,000).

Noted one impressed friend: "Dennis is the medicine that Liz needs to complete her cure."*

Elizabeth's Gstaad home—Chalet Ariel—was the site of several happy family gatherings. The five-bedroom wooden villa with its long balconies was decorated with elaborate evergreen wreaths, satin bows, garlands, and plenty of romantic clumps of mistletoe. A tall tree covered with twinkling lights and shining ornaments was in one corner of the big living room with its huge windows overlooking one of the resort's major ski runs. Scattered under the tree's sweeping branches were dozens of presents, many of them wrapped in lavender paper with purple ribbons.

Everything about the entire holiday season was absolutely wonderful for Elizabeth. It was hard to believe

---

* Elizabeth's only remaining vice is Salem cigarettes. "She's smoking nonstop," said one friend. Elizabeth admits to a tobacco addiction, saying that it began in earnest at the Betty Ford Center, where she'd never seen so much smoke outside of a three-alarm fire.

that only a short year before she had been a pudgy butterball, sitting with her mother and Victor Luna in a cafeteria of the Betty Ford Center grimly eating sliced turkey and cranberries.

After returning from Gstaad, Elizabeth suddenly began to look at Stein in a different light. His jocular manner suddenly seemed coarse, and the strength she had once admired was now turning boorish. The Stein mannerism which annoyed her the most was his well-oiled tongue. A gabby and open person, Stein thought nothing about telling friends exactly what was going on between him and Elizabeth—any time of day or night.

Because she is so often in the public eye, Elizabeth jealously guards her private time. She became furious at overhearing him tell a friend on the phone that she was cooking dinner for him. Another time she was livid after he told a group of people that she changes her mind every ten minutes. He also began telling gossip columnists intimate tidbits about their romance.

Soon after that, Elizabeth confided to a friend, "It's not going to last. Dennis is a sweet guy, but he is driving me nuts. My friends are laughing at me, and if this goes on, my fans will think I'm a fool, too."

In late January 1985, the clouds had completely parted. A wiser Elizabeth floated back to earth and returned Stein's engagement ring.

"I think I'm finally growing up, and about time," Elizabeth revealed to a journalist. "I will marry once more, but *only* once more."

# Chapter Eight

*"I'm having fun!"—Elizabeth Taylor*

WHEN Elizabeth gave Dennis Stein back his engagement ring, it was almost as if she'd been let out of the chains of bondage which had imprisoned her since she was eighteen. For the first time in her life, she realized that (gasp!) it was okay to be without a steady man. Being single really wasn't the next worst thing to eternal damnation. It really was quite enjoyable.

Determined to put all the sorrow and hard times behind her, Elizabeth dove into a whirlwind of dating as gleefully as any spunky teenager. In fact, it almost looked as though she was trying to make up for all the fun she'd missed out on when she was fifteen and sixteen—and busily turning out several MGM flicks each year.

And, like any teenager, she discovered the uninhibited good times available at rock concerts. Halfway through his opening number of "Born to Run," Bruce Springsteen barely noticed a group of VIPs who slipped into a special block of reserved seats. Sitting next to hairstylist Jose Ebar was a slender woman sporting a flashy New Wave outfit and a Day-Glo yellow punked-out hairstyle so tall it blocked the view of the people in the row behind. One guest decided that the person under all that hair must be "either a Twisted Sister or a star of one of those punk rock videos." Until she went backstage during intermission to sip a diet soda from the can and nibble on the fresh fruit, raw vegetables, and cold cut sandwiches spread out on an uncovered folding table, no one realized that this punk princess was formerly the Queen of the Nile.

A short time later, she showed up at the concert of another dedicated, but decidedly raucous, devotee of her favorite color of purple—Prince. Still wearing her punk leathers, this time she was spotted in a black spiked wig and wearing a flower behind one ear. Catching sight of another member of the American royal family, Prince leaned down from the stage and grandly offered her a single red rose, which she graciously accepted with a big smile.

Then the Grammy Award–winning singer decided to pay Elizabeth a visit and personally thank her for attending his concert, but he did it with an indelicacy that is difficult to imagine. Prince arrived at Elizabeth's Bel Air home accompanied by his father and four bodyguards. After the singer and his dad entered the house, one of the burly strongarms stood guard by the door while the other three searched through the bushes.

An alarmed Elizabeth caught sight of their actions and demanded to know what the hell was going on. She later told friends that she'd asked Prince, "Did you think I hired assassins?"

One rock friendship which flourished much longer was between Elizabeth and Michael Jackson. After attending his concert with Dennis Stein, Elizabeth was struck by the beauty and sensitivity of the young singer. She mentioned her interest in him to mutual friend Jackie Onassis, and a meeting was soon set up.

The soft-spoken singer's gentle manners were intriguing to Elizabeth, who has been known to surround herself with boisterous he-man types. After their initial meeting, Jackson and Elizabeth discovered all the things they had in common. Since they both have been celebrities since early childhood and have never been able to live a "normal" life out of the limelight, they found a kindred spirit in each other.

Before long, they began going out on the town together, Elizabeth wrapped up in her luscious fur coats and Jackson sporting his then-trademark Sergeant Pepper–style sequined jackets and dark shades. Hand in hand, laughing and smiling, they were spotted at awards banquets, the opening day of Hollywood Park Race Track (where she laughed loudly at his jokes and playfully hit him on the head with her rolled-up program), movie premieres, parties, and various other show-business functions.

As their friendship grew, so did Jackson's infatuation with Elizabeth and with everything about her. Friends say he devoted a room in his home especially to her, filling it with mementos of her long career. The lavender-hued décor featured special wallpaper printed with her smiling face. Adorning the walls are large, full-color photos in ornate gold frames depicting the star in her major film roles—Cleopatra, Velvet, Maggie the Cat, and more. A bookshelf is piled high with every book that even mentions her name, and a large-screen TV plays her movies nonstop, twenty-four hours a day, even if the room is empty.

Naturally, Elizabeth was extremely flattered by Jackson's obvious adoration. In turn, she fixed up a room in her home for the singer. Some sketches that Jackson made of her are hanging on the walls, along with photos of his other favorite movie stars, including Marilyn Monroe. She gave him a key to her house and told him to come anytime he needed a quiet place to relax.

As the months passed, Jackson began to languish when he wasn't seeing her. He told one friend that he'd stopped going out with his former escort, Brooke Shields, because: "Brooke is a nice girl, but she's no Elizabeth Taylor. That's the kind of lady I want to be seen with."

According to friends, Jackson doesn't like to associate with people who aren't on a par with him. "Since he feels he's a legend, he'll only be seen with other legends, like Elizabeth Taylor."

Their friendship may also have partly precipitated the pop star's break from his Jehovah's Witness religion. The Witnesses are not allowed to celebrate birthdays, and photos of Jackson at Elizabeth's birthday parties ran in papers around the world.

Eventually, his great admiration for her grew into love, and one source said he even asked her to marry him. A shocked Elizabeth tried to say no without shattering the sensitive young man, and she has cooled their friendship considerably since then.

Elizabeth's other suitors have been far more conventional. Soon after breaking up with Dennis Stein,

Elizabeth was seen dining in Beverly Hills with Neil Papiano, a partner in a Los Angeles law firm who is two years younger than she.

Papiano's firm represents Hollywood Park Race Track, which is where they met. The pair was spotted at the track's Breeders' Cup Ball and dining at Chasen's, but Papiano denied any serious romance. "It's presumptuous to say I'm even a friend," he once said.

Wealthy Miami horse breeder Ed Seltzer was another of Elizabeth's beaus whom she met through friends at Hollywood Park. The Park's chairman of the board, Marje Everett, introduced them, and Seltzer invited Elizabeth to join him in Miami after their second meeting. Because the star was suffering from her recurrent back problems, she couldn't fly on a commercial aircraft. Kindhearted Seltzer flew her down in his private plane which has a bed and sofa on it.

Elizabeth was so thrilled by his thoughtfulness that she began telling friends: "Ed is my Prince Charming."

Returning the compliment, Seltzer called her "one of the most exciting women I have ever met in my life. I think she is wonderful."

Another man who thought Elizabeth was pretty special was record producer Richard Perry. He stuck close by her side and was great in helping her get over her grief when Rock Hudson died.

With all that wild dating, one would expect a few flashes of jealousy, and since the object of all that attention was the famous Elizabeth Taylor, those flashes weren't mere sparks.

Nine months after she broke off her engagement

with Stein, he attended a celebrity-laced party for singer Whitney Houston held at New York's Palladium. Spotting Carl Bernstein at the bar, Stein rushed over.

Immediately, the party's hostess, Nikki Haskell, was alerted to the problem. "I was talking to someone when my boyfriend told me, 'You'd better go get Dennis—he's in a fight!'

"When I got there Carl and Dennis were standing in the disco's Mike Todd Room—which is pretty ironic because the room is named after one of Liz Taylor's husbands."

Apparently, Stein had heard from friends that Bernstein was doing an investigation into his personal matters, trying to dig up the dirt that would prevent him from ever wooing Elizabeth back. But the actress has remained friends with the investigative reporter to this day.

The year 1985 was one when the world welcomed back a beautiful new Elizabeth with open arms. In January, she was awarded the Cecil B. deMille Award by the Hollywood Foreign Press Association at the forty-second annual Golden Globe Awards.

It is a prestigious award, one which honors the recipient's lifetime of achievement in the film industry. Past winners have included Paul Newman, Walt Disney, Bob Hope, Bette Davis, James Stewart, and Judy Garland.

In addition to honoring her contributions to the film world, it was a salute to "Miss Taylor's resilience and courage as a human being, thereby providing inspiration and hope to others, as well as her generous participation in charity activities," said the HFPA.

"It's amazing," she said, hugging the statue. "And to be given it by the press . . . that's *really* amazing."

When she was honored as "Humanitarian of the Year" by L.A.'s Starlight Foundation in late January, she bid $2,000 to spend a day and have dinner with Superbowl MVP Joe Montana. Her accepted bid turned into another dream date.

A month later, she looked ravishing at President Reagan's Inaugural Ball and danced all night. Later in the year, she was honored at the American Academy of Achievement's twenty-fourth annual "Salute to Excellence."

One of the world's finest honors was presented to her that September in Paris—she was named a Commander of Arts and Letters, France's highest cultural distinction. Presenter of the award, French Minister of Culture M. Jack Lang, was nervous when Elizabeth hadn't yet shown up an hour after the ceremony was scheduled to begin—but when she finally did arrive, she looked so ravishing that all was quickly forgiven.

Of course, her life since leaving the Betty Ford Center wasn't only a mad rush of romantic socializing. Close friends say there were many lonely moments when Elizabeth desperately wished for a seventh permanent shoulder to cry on.

Instead of wallowing in the despair that occasionally hit her, Elizabeth decided to forget her pain by helping other people get rid of their own problems.

The crusade she jumped into, naturally, was helping friends to end their own addictions to alcohol and drugs. Although her first attempt—with Peter Lawford—had a sad ending, her second try was a smashing success.

119

Six months after becoming sober, Elizabeth got a call from Lorna Luft. Liza Minnelli, the half-sister of Luft and a dear friend of Elizabeth, was suffering from her own addiction to pills and booze.

"I was just a lump, a hopeless, miserable lump," is how Minnelli describes herself at that time.

Luft didn't know how to handle the problem and needed advice. She poured out a story which was all too familiar to Elizabeth.

The singer had been taking Valium and drinking heavily for many years. Already, she had fallen into the typical alcoholic patterns: the hospitalizations for unexplained illnesses, missing work (performances in the Broadway musical *The Rink*), and serious marital problems.

To make matters worse, Minnelli had a history of substance abuse in her family. Her mother—Judy Garland—had admitted by the time she was thirty that she was addicted to booze and drugs, but she believed that "Alcoholics Anonymous will never do me any good." She once attended a meeting of the A.A. while clutching a silver flask. At another A.A. meeting, Garland had the shakes so badly she sneaked out early to get a drink.

For years people had been telling Minnelli that her extraordinary talents and meteoric rise to fame was just like her mother's—and that she was going to die a drunk like mom, as well. Minnelli could see the destructive patterns growing within her and decided to put them to an end. She had nothing left to lose—husband Mark Gero was already so disgusted with her abuses that he'd walked out, and they were on the verge of a divorce. Plus, her work in *The Rink* had been dismissed by the critics. She frequently partied all night, all over New York. Because of her late working hours, she says she reached parties at a time when people were already smashed, but she always caught up quickly.

Elizabeth told Luft to go ahead and tell her half-sister that she needed to check immediately into a substance-abuse program. Then she anxiously waited by the phone to hear Minnelli's decision and offer any moral support she could.

After that, Elizabeth packed her bags, determined to visit her chum. It was going to be very hard for Minnelli to break successfully out of the vicious cycle of addiction, and Elizabeth wanted to give her all the help possible.

Encouraged by frequent visits and calls from Elizabeth and Luft, Minnelli completed the treatment and returned to New York. Elizabeth had taken her assistance one step further, and counseled Minnelli to try working things out with her husband.

After that, the star called Gero and begged him to give her friend the love and reassurance Minnelli would need to stick to the strait and narrow. Elizabeth had told friends she really wanted Minnelli to stay with her for a few weeks—partly to ease her own loneliness and partly to help the singer over the rough parts of her reentry into society—but unselfishly she insisted that Minnelli return to her husband after leaving the center.

Gero admitted that he'd been part of his wife's problems, and the shock made him realize his own addictions and check into a treatment program. "I was a drinking, drugging, misogynist macho dago jerk," he was quoted as saying later.

For a few months it seemed like Minnelli was sticking to her vows, but suddenly Elizabeth heard rumors to the contrary. Anxious to see what the situation really was, Elizabeth went to the bar at Le Mondrian Hotel in West Hollywood where Minnelli was throwing a party to celebrate the opening night of her pianist pal, Michael Feinstein.

A stunned Elizabeth saw Minnelli holding a glass of wine. She immediately took the singer aside and began bawling her out for falling off the wagon. As soon as Minnelli's other close friends—Feinstein, ex-husband Jack Haley, Jr., and Minnelli's personal physician—saw what was going on, they gathered around. Each one told Minnelli that he was horribly worried about her, and if she kept on drinking she was going to kill herself.

A tearful Minnelli ran off to the ladies' room, but when she returned everyone could see the difference in her. She agreed to seek treatment again; and on her doctor's advice, entered the stricter Hazelden Clinic in Center City, Minnesota.

This time, when Minnelli emerged she had finally kicked alcohol and pills for good. Even when she can't sleep or her back hurts, "Aspirin is the most I take . . . and somehow it hurts less," Minnelli said. "Elizabeth was saying that, too, that her back hurts less without all that medication they used to put her on."

For the first time, Minnelli isn't viewing her mother as her only role model; at last she's looking at her other strong parent, movie director Vincente Minnelli who directed Elizabeth in *Father of the Bride*. She's physically stronger than ever, and she's nearly back down to what she weighed when she was in *Cabaret.* Her good health has even improved her voice—it's stronger and capable of richer tones.

"My marriage is important to me. My health is important to me," she says softly. "My marriage is so good, it's stupid."

Minnelli stresses that Elizabeth's successful fight against substance abuse was what helped her to get straight. "Lorna and I both commented on how remarkable Elizabeth looked when she came out of the Betty Ford Center in January, how healthy and at peace she seemed to be. At the time, Elizabeth had said she didn't really know what her problem was until she got there. She only knew the symptoms."

A delighted Elizabeth toasted her friend's newfound serenity with a bubbling glass of Perrier and joked about her prominent role in Minnelli's change. "When I put my mind to a goal, I achieve it. Just iron determination, come hell or high water—that's me!

"If I can be an example to other women when it comes to those difficult times, then it makes everything so worthwhile," Elizabeth told a reporter.

Minnelli is also preaching the sober gospel now. It's so much *hipper* being straight," she says with a big smile.

"Remember how great Elizabeth looked at Giants Stadium on Liberty Weekend? You know what? If you want what she's got, you can get it. It's very important to know that. If you want what I've got, you can get it. We can't all look like Elizabeth Taylor, darn it, but we can look like that inside.

"The biggest thing is just keeping it . . . simple."

Determined to help as many people as possible, Elizabeth went on to make a TV movie called *From This Day Forward* in which she played the part of a drunken housewife and mother battling to get off booze.

"My own personal experiences are helping me in this role," she said.

"In preparing for this movie there have been many times when my eyes have filled with tears as I remember my own personal anguishes and fears."

Elizabeth insisted that she couldn't just "sit back and be smug and proud of myself because I was able to get help in time. Alcoholism is tragic and disastrous for everyone, but it's especially tough on women.

"I believe God wants me to help other women facing the problems. If only a few women in the United States are helped by this film, then I know it was worth all the time and effort."

# Chapter Nine

*"I'm deathly afraid of the surgeon's knife, but
I just can't stand the pain anymore."*
—Elizabeth Taylor

AFTER long years reigning as the undisputed queen of the silver screen, it seemed as though Elizabeth had decided to conquer the boob tube as well.

"She will now do anything she thinks has merit—television, stage, or movies," said a friend of her manager, Roger Wall. "She's determined to be the busiest actress in Hollywood."

Many people thought Elizabeth would choose to saunter down the nighttime soap opera route followed by so many former screen stars. Adding up the tremendous figures such roles pay, anyone can see why big stars are so easily lured into playing even a minor character on a soap.

For a while rumors flew wild across Hollywood that Elizabeth was going to step into the role of superbitch Alexis on *Dynasty*. The actress playing the part—Joan Collins—was refusing to work unless her $50,000-a-week salary was doubled. But Elizabeth quickly squelched the talk, saying she had never even considered taking the role.

Together with Carol Burnett, Elizabeth made a movie in Toronto for HBO called *Between Friends*, for a paycheck estimated at $500,000. She enjoyed the experience tremendously and got one of the biggest laughs of her life from a writer friend of her comedienne co-star.

Since Elizabeth's birthday fell on a filming day, Burnett threw her a party. One guest who flew in for the occasion was Hollywood writer Kenny Solms.

He handed Elizabeth a card and told her, "I didn't know what to get for the woman who has everything. So I want you to choose something yourself. Get yourself something special." Inside the envelope was a check for ten dollars. Elizabeth laughed until she cried and hasn't ever cashed the check.

During this period of working hard on TV, one small part of her theatrical past came back to haunt her.

In 1983, actress Cicely Tyson demanded arbitration from the Actors Equity/Producers League to settle a disagreement she had with Elizabeth and producer Zev Bufman. Tyson was promised a total of $750,000 in a "pay or play" contract for the stage production of *The Corn is Green*.

The play was the second in a joint venture between Elizabeth and Bufman to produce three plays under their production company, The Elizabeth Taylor Theatre Group. The Burton-Taylor-reuniting *Private Lives* was the first play in the series, and *Inherit the Wind* was to have been the third.

Tyson had been fired when the management felt she breached her contract after she missed one performance and allegedly "failed to follow the director's advice." Tyson was asking for the balance payment of $625,000. Her contract specifically stated that any dispute be arbitrated rather than go through the courts. Actors Equity/Producers League vindicated her when the grievance committee unanimously decided that Tyson hadn't breached her contract and ordered that she be paid the balance due under the stage portion of the contract.

Tyson was "pleased" by the hearing's outcome, but still held out for both the stage and TV portions, wishing to "compel Ms. Taylor and Bufman to honor their commitment." She had stated that her dismissal stemmed from the producers' wish to save money on a flop—not from any misconduct on her part.

In spring 1985, she was awarded the remaining $625,000 by the American Arbitrator Association. The actress publicly regretted being forced to take legal action, but added she was satisfied with the settlement.

Elizabeth firmly left the theatrical world behind and entered a new facet of the TV industry when she took on a guest appearance in the miniseries *North and South.* In her cameo role she played Madam Conti, the owner of a New Orleans bordello. One reviewer said she was hardly on camera long enough to be recognized. Even such a tiny part can bring in big bucks, however; reports said she was handed nearly $100,000 for her work.

The Civil War drama was filmed in Charleston, S.C., and the mayor invited the actress to dinner with all the most important people in town. Elizabeth flew there in her private plane outfitted with comfortable camel-leather chairs.

The delicious southern-style cooking proved to be her downfall, and she indulged herself in the fried chicken, mashed potatoes, biscuits, and gravy she so adores. One guest saw her take a huge slice of mud pie (mocha ice cream on a chocolate cookie crust topped with hot fudge, whipped cream, and pecans). The next day she looked in the mirror and said, "Oh, I look so fat!" and went right back on her diet.

The food wasn't her biggest problem with the miniseries, however. Her costume was an elaborate low-cut, off-the-shoulder black satin dress trimmed with velvet and lace netting. Not only was it so tight that she literally had to be laced into it, but with its hoops and dozens of petticoats, the dress weighed a spine-crushing fifty pounds.

Dragging around all that excess weight for up to sixteen hours a day caused her so much back pain that she was soon rushed to St. John's Hospital. "It hurt when they squeezed me into it, and a day or two later I was in agony," she told a pal. "Whoever would have thought a dress would put me in the hospital?"

According to her stand-in, Suzanne Gundlach, "The corset is absolutely the most uncomfortable thing you can imagine. I had to wear one and, believe me, it is no fun.

"I know she was all trussed up in that thing and on her feet for at least ten hours. I never heard her complain, but I know it must have been pulling at her back muscles, because I could feel it on mine.

"She stood the pain for two weeks, before her doctor advised her that it wasn't going to go away on its own."

The agonizing injury was a terrible setback for Elizabeth, but she refused to use it as an excuse to slide back into her old habits.

Back in the hospital, she refused the painkillers doctors were pushing on her. "Since my addiction problems, I refuse to take any drugs to help me—but I'm in pain," she told a friend who visited her.

When the star was at St. John's, the specialists did everything in their power to make her more comfortable. She was given heat treatments to loosen and relax her back muscles. After that she was placed in traction for about fifteen minutes. This involved lying on a special table with a strap around her head and chin. The strap is connected to a pulley and weight contraption which slowly stretches out the spine and muscles in the back until the "slipped disc" slides back into place. Both treatments were followed with a fifteen-minute back massage to ease any discomfort the traction had caused.

Four weeks of these treatments failed to bring about the hoped-for results. Elizabeth was still suffering from such acute pain that she was forced to lie down all the time. Sitting up or moving in any way was sheer torture. She couldn't even talk on the phone.

"There have been times when I undergo extreme torture if I so much as take a step," she says. "And there are other times when I'm absolutely helpless in bed, unable to make any move."

During the long weeks she spent convalescing, Elizabeth had a videotape recorder brought into her room and took a little trip down memory lane by playing all the old movies she'd starred in, as well as the ones starring Richard Burton.

Friends said she became melancholy, remembering

the high points of their life and love together. Her depression grew even deeper because none of her current or former beaus bothered to stop by the hospital or send flowers. Her only visitors were old, true friends such as Rock Hudson and Roddy McDowall. Her children sent beautiful baskets of exotic flowers, but Elizabeth was crushed that none of her lovers had sent as much as a daisy.

Most of all, she was disheartened by the reports from her doctors. Many back specialists were called in, and each one told her the same thing: she needed surgery to correct the problems she'd lived with since falling off Pi during the filming of *National Velvet* in 1944.

That was the last thing Elizabeth wanted to hear. She felt that she'd been sliced up by enough surgeons in her lifetime and wasn't ready to dive back under the scalpel. Her nineteen major operations included her famous tracheotomy, a hysterectomy, removal of an ovarian cyst, removal of a piece of flint—then, years later, some metal dust—from her eye, three cesarean sections, an appendectomy, oral surgery, and other gynecological surgery. Her back injury was compounded when she was hit with a door during the filming of *The Last Time I Saw Paris* and when she fell down the steps on a yacht just before marrying Mike Todd. Both occasions had demanded immediate hospitalization.

"If Liz opens a can of beer, she cuts herself. If there's a chair on the set, she'll fall over it," director Richard Brooks said when working with her years before. For decades she was known as the worst insurance liability ever to set foot on a movie set.

Elizabeth was scared stiff of having another operation, telling friends, "It's so complicated in your back —it's like a brain operation, so much to go wrong. One slip and I could be paralyzed . . . or in a wheelchair."

In addition to all of her own pain and suffering, she's seen just as much agony in her loved ones. The problems ex-husband Richard Burton suffered after his own back surgery were still fresh in her mind.

Said a close friend, "After Richard underwent spinal surgery, his health deteriorated considerably—and that memory haunts Liz like a ghost. She doesn't want to end up like him."

Despite Elizabeth's constant prayers, the pain did not abate after a year, and the actress was forced to choose the spinal surgery. According to Dr. Martin Weiss, professor and chairman of the department of neurosurgery at the University of California, a bone graft from her hip was used to fuse together two or more vertebrae in her back. This eliminates the pain caused when the discs rub together.

Despite her terror of having another operation, Elizabeth decided that even facing the knife was preferable to more suffering. Just before having the operation, she told a friend, "One day I'm fine, and the next day I'm in agonizing pain."

Dr. Neil Kahanovitz, chief of back surgery at the Hospital for Joint Diseases-Orthopedic Institute in New York, admitted that the surgery Elizabeth had chosen to undergo wasn't without risks. "You can have problems with the anesthetic, you can have infection— anything can go wrong," he said. The spine has "nerves that are very susceptible to injury."

Kahanovitz admitted that there was a chance that the surgery might not help Elizabeth and might even make her worse. In about fifteen percent of cases, the surgery doesn't stop the pain and "in a very few, it will worsen."

Fortunately, Elizabeth's lifelong luck held out. The operation did no further damage and has actually relieved some of the excruciating pain, allowing her to live a normal—if cautious—life again.

A physical therapist comes to her home to help her with swimming exercises that keep her back muscles supple. Elizabeth also finds that sleeping in the fetal position—on her side with her legs drawn up—on a firm mattress also relieves some of the discomfort.

She always carries a special pillow for her back, and sits on a straight chair with the pillow placed against the small of her back. Elizabeth also wears a special tightly laced corset to keep her back in the proper alignment (and it is also part of the secret of her tiny waistline).

Months later, a radiant Elizabeth and close friends Burt Bacharach and Carole Bayer Sager watched the actress's first thoroughbred racehorse—Basic Image—gallop down the dirt track at Hollywood Park. Resplendent in a baggy yellow V-necked shirt over a lime-green miniskirt, yellow fishnet stockings, and yellow pumps, she shouted "Go! Go!" and waved wildly as world-famous jockey Willie Shoemaker drove Basic Image toward home.

Wearing her bright cerise and chartreuse diamond silks, Shoemaker flashed by at the head of the pack but was edged out by Variety Express's nose just before the wire. Elizabeth audibly groaned "Awww" after the loss, but never lost her cheerful smile as she bent to kiss the jockey and promised her guests that the horse would be a winner the next time.

Why not? His owner certainly is.

# Chapter Ten

*"We're just a close, happy family."*
—Michael Wilding, Jr.

THEY'VE been darlings and devils, droll and delightful, handsome handfuls and sweetly saucy. Like all kids, they've made their mother swell with pride, laugh with delight, and tear at her hair with anguish. Despite the fact that the mother is none other than Elizabeth Taylor, at home she was the one they ran to with scraped fingers which needed to be kissed, problems which needed solving, and funny stories to share.

They may have lived their lives in a fishbowl of media attention and world scrutiny, yet that isn't how Elizabeth's children remember growing up. Instead of the incessant clamor of the reporters, the camera lenses pressed up against their living-room windows, and the constant need for bodyguards, Michael and Christopher Wilding, Liza Todd, and Maria Burton only remember the warm, loving times with their famous parents.

They claim that being shunted constantly around the world and learning in private classes with tutors never made them long for a permanent home. Never do they speak publicly about their parents' drinking, arguing, or the tragedies which marred their early years.

And, despite the frequent turnovers in male authority figures and their three different fathers, each child grew up as a completely separate and equal person in their mother's eyes—each one getting his or her fair share of affection, treats, or scoldings.

Elizabeth has always adored children and been a concerned, loving mother. Even when she married Nicky Hilton, admittedly as "a terribly immature girl . . . I was dying to have children."

Three months after marrying Michael Wilding, Elizabeth got pregnant with Michael, Jr., and two years later Christopher came along. Pregnancy was the most miraculous experience of her life. Trying to explain it, she said: "Procreation is the greatest miracle of all, and you are participating in it, contributing to it. . . .You feel an affinity with all the vast things in the world since time began. And you feel so small. Because you are such a crucial part of such a miracle, I think every mother when she's carrying a baby must feel tremendously important. I know I've never felt so important in my life. I've never felt so beautiful."

However, her next experience with pregnancy wasn't quite such a joyful one. Since the reconstruction surgery on her back had been done such a short time after Liza was conceived, her doctors thought that the pressure from the baby would push the newly formed bones out of place and cripple her. They urged her to abort the fetus and she firmly opposed them.

The doctors designed a back brace with elastic gussets over her stomach to make room for the baby, and at one point the brace pushed Liza so far up under her ribs that Elizabeth's heart was moved over a couple of inches and she felt faint all the time.

She nearly lost the baby three times. Once she was crossing the Atlantic and the doctor on the boat was so inept that Elizabeth felt that "he thought babies came out of your nose." The labor pains stopped by the time she got to New York, but two weeks later Elizabeth's pulse was so high that the doctors decided to perform the cesarean early.

Elizabeth Frances (Liza) was stillborn. Mike Todd was told, "Your wife, we think, will be all right, but the baby's dead." A resuscitationist in the delivery room worked on her for fourteen and one-half minutes, then the four-pound child finally took her first gasp of air.

When Todd went in to see the tiny baby, she made a little movement of her arm, and her father was utterly convinced that she was waving at him. He immediately went to Tiffany's and bought a little gold hairbrush for her and had engraved on it: "Dear Liza, I wanted to buy you platinum, but Mommy says I shouldn't spoil you."

Although Elizabeth couldn't have any more babies after Liza, she still wanted a child to bind her closer to her next husband, Eddie Fisher. Eventually, little Maria did serve just that purpose for her mother, but with a different husband, Richard Burton.

After deciding she wanted to adopt a baby, Elizabeth told her good friend Maria Schell about her plan. Schell put an ad into a German newspaper, saying that a wealthy foreign couple wanted to give a good home to a child. A poor couple who already had two daughters and who were living in a nine-by-fifteen-foot room, brought in their three-day-old child Petra.

"I thought if Petra could have a better life in another home I would not stand in her way," the infant's mother said later. "I wanted to give her a chance."

Elizabeth first saw the baby propped up on a couple of pillows in the bottom of a wicker laundry basket. She picked her up and was appalled by the obvious malnutrition the child was suffering from, and the abscesses all over her body. Elizabeth had three days before she had to fly to Italy for *Cleopatra* and asked if she could care for the baby.

At first Petra wouldn't smile or cry, but before Elizabeth had to leave for Rome she says the little girl "began to awaken and soon became a laughing, gurgling baby who let her needs be known. That swift change made me love her desperately."

Then they took a bath together, and while bouncing the child up and down Elizabeth noticed that her left hip would collapse completely under her. Although Schell and all the lawyers arranging the adoption showed Elizabeth pictures of other children—and urged her to select another, "perfect" baby—the star already loved this one like her own and decided she'd do everything within her power to correct the child's deformity.

Petra was renamed Maria—after her benefactor Maria Schell—and began living a life she remembers as right out of the book *The Ugly Duckling*. "Suddenly, instead of the four bare walls of an orphanage room, I had homes all over the world. In place of the nurses who hid my ugliness, I had a family who adored me—a mother and father, two elder brothers . . . and a big sister to look up to and admire."

Before Elizabeth married Burton and set up homes in Switzerland and Puerto Vallarta, the children lived a nomadic life, moving from hotel to hotel, because she never liked being parted from them if she could help it. Sometimes Michael and Christopher were sent to stay with their father (who later married Margaret Leighton). Elizabeth was traveling so much to make movies and with Mike Todd to promote *Around the World in 80 Days* that the kids were left behind with nurses more and more frequently. Before splitting up with Fisher, she did try to create a semblance of a family life.

Outsiders didn't see her attempts at making a normal life, nor did they view the love and attention she lavished on her children when they were together. After *le scandale* flashed around the world, the Vatican newspaper called her a bad mother and claimed that the German adoption agency letting her have Maria was remiss in its responsibility. An article in *L'Osservatore della Domenica*, the Vatican weekly, stated, "Was it not better to entrust this girl to an honest bricklayer and to a modest housewife rather than to you, my dear lady, and to your fourth ex-husband?"

Despite this global condemnation, her children didn't see her in that light. During the time their mother was moping around, trying to hide that she was "dying inside" from not being able to get together with Richard Burton, the children did all they could to help her. Michael wrote her letters saying, "I know it's going to be all right, Mama," and Christopher once told her, "I prayed to God last night that you and Richard would be married."

Her children began to accept Richard before the couple married, and after the wedding, grew to love and respect him as the head of the household. When the teasing and roughhousing got out of hand, "Dad drew himself up to his full height and delivered a lecture to us in the sort of ringing tones an actor would use for a Shakespearean soliloquy," Maria remembers.

Maria stresses how close she was with the man who gave her his last name. "Although I wasn't Richard Burton's child—wasn't even his choice as an adopted child—I've always felt so close to him that . . . he's the only dad I've ever had."

In fact, Burton wasn't terribly keen on adoption at all and vetoed the idea when Elizabeth suggested they adopt a boy to carry on the Burton name. "We have the money to indulge ourselves with pets," he said, "but we can take no risk at all with a child that is going to bear our name."

Despite his not wanting another adopted child, Burton loved Maria deeply. He insisted that Maria be treated by Welsh doctors, and completely oversaw the various operations on her hip. Once he wanted to show her that a blood test wouldn't hurt, so he had the doctor draw some of his own blood first. She was in various body casts for five years, and when the doctors finally took all the pins out of her leg, Burton put them into a jar and kept them until his death.

When she thinks back on all the years she spent in hospitals, she doesn't remember the pain. Her recollections are of the smiling face and kindness of her father.

Maria was slow to develop, perhaps because of all her physical problems. She simply says she was taking everything in. But once she was healed, she began to dash madly about, making up for lost time by investigating all the closets and corners she'd never seen.

She began speaking then, too. Her first word, "Mama," melted Elizabeth's heart. Maria laughs that her parents probably secretly breathed a sigh of relief, thinking, "Ah, she's intelligent after all!"

The shy one of the bunch, Maria always woke up first, and she says she hardly ever left her room as a young child. Burton bought her a huge doll house and boxes of furniture and instructed her to completely redecorate the house every day before anyone else woke up. "I was usually in a panic, thinking I wouldn't finish, until Liza woke up and came downstairs to help," Maria says.

Elizabeth's youngest daughter feels that Burton's idea of sending all the kids off to different boarding schools actually helped to make them grow closer as a family because siblings who are together day after day fight more. "When we'd come home on vacations, there they'd be, sitting in the living room of our chalet, Mum in one chair, Dad in the other, each reading a book. We'd all catch up with each other's news, then go to the kitchen and cook dinner together."

Worried that their life-style wasn't healthful, Elizabeth once asked her children if they'd like it better if she weren't a famous film actress. They told her they were proud of her and wouldn't want things any other way.

The overbearing aspects of their parents' fame did creep in, however. Sometimes Michael or Christopher was teased that "Your mother's a big, fat movie star, and she's got big bosoms," forcing them to use their small fists to defend her honor and came home many times with bloody noses or black eyes. Maria had a prized Polaroid camera her father had given her, and one day opened her desk at school to find it broken to bits.

Once an annoying female reporter followed Maria and her school pals on skis and later stuck a telephoto lens into their living room window. When she was thirteen, the Burtons split up, and one London paper printed a story that Maria's natural parents were offering $5,000 to get her back. The girl was so disgusted by the article, she decided never to meet the man and woman responsible for her birth—and continued loving the man and woman who were giving her such a wonderful life.

The child who gave Elizabeth the most trouble while growing up was Michael. (He dropped using *Junior* after his father died in 1979.) "I wasn't a good student," he admits. "I blame it on all the moving around and changing schools. They sent me to the best schools, but I was asked to leave two of them."

Although his mother called him "terribly deep and sensitive" as a child, Michael went through a teenage rebellion at his parents' ostentatious style of living and attempted to drop out of society.

When Michael was fifteen, Burton complained, "Our son is a hippie. His hair lies on his shoulders, and we can't keep him in school. I tell Elizabeth we should do one of two things—ignore him or kick the living daylights out of him."

A year later, Michael was asked not to return to his exclusive boarding school—Millfield—so Elizabeth sent him and Christopher off to live with her brother Howard, who was then working in Hawaii as a professor of oceanography. Michael met Beth Clutter, a sweet young keypunch operator two years his senior, on the beach. Together they took off to explore exotic lands such as India and—like so many other young people of their generation—tried to find life's missing ingredients in Eastern philosophies.

Just before his eighteenth birthday in 1970, Michael and Beth decided to wed. He wore a red caftan and his hair flowed down to his shoulders. Elizabeth gave them a honeymoon at the Dorchester Hotel's bridal suite and Burton bought them a house in London. A short while later Beth informed them that she was pregnant. When little Leyla was born, her forty-year-old Grandmother Elizabeth was "delighted."

The camera assistant job his mother had gotten for him didn't suit Michael's artistic sensibilities, so he took his family to live in a commune in Wales.

Burton was furious, ranting, "I made it up, and Michael is trying to make it down. I try not to interfere, but I still get goddamned mad. When I think what it took to climb out."

Beth was forced to cook and clean for the other commune members as well as her own family, and the burden proved too much for her. She went to stay with Elizabeth in London for a while until the star's lifestyle again rubbed her the wrong way, at which point she returned to her parents' home in Portland, Oregon.

"My husband would not fulfill his obligations to my child, which is also his child. I did not ask for anything for myself, just for our baby," Beth said at the time.

Elizabeth, who had been sending support checks, cut Beth off when the divorce was filed. "Elizabeth was angry with me over the phone when I called her, and she said she would never see me again," Beth said.

"And yet, when we were married in London, she told me she would always help no matter what happened. I was to regard her as my second mother, and I would always be her daughter."

Michael was spending all his time playing music, hoping to make it into the rock'n'roll circuit. He eventually played saxophone with a few bands in Europe.

In the late 1970's, Michael finally came to terms with his abilities and began taking acting lessons in England and in Los Angeles. He'd always been fascinated when Burton would act out entire Shakespearean plays at home and even memorized some soliloquies himself as a child.*

As an adult, Michael didn't need anyone's help to get acting jobs. His inherent good looks—a combination of the best of Elizabeth and Michael Wilding—combined with his natural talent to land him jobs as Jesus Christ on the TV miniseries *A.D.*, some off-Broadway plays, and a continuing part on the daytime soap *The Guiding Light*.

He learned his craft at the feet of masters. About his

---

* When Elizabeth had gotten some offers from friends to put Michael in movies, she turned them down cold, saying, "One ex–child actor in the family is enough."

mother he says, "I think she's a very fine actress. I'm sure I've learned from her—just by watching her over the years."

His interest in becoming an actor, however, stemmed from observing his dad and Richard Burton. "With his knowledge of literature, poetry, and the theater, he [Burton] taught us a lot of things," Michael says.

On August 26, 1982, a very handsome Michael donned a white tuxedo and married Brooke Palance— the daughter of Jack Palance—in a traditional ceremony. Elizabeth Taylor's "bad boy" had finally settled down to become a respectable man.

When his proud mother came to see him act in the Riverwest Theater's off-Broadway production of *Dead Wrong,* she did everything possible not to steal any of her son's glory. Elizabeth and Maria entered the theater without any fanfare and quietly took seats in the rear. Later she let Brooke hostess the small cast party, waiting until the next night to treat her son and daughter-in-law to a quiet dinner.

"Our relationship is a good one," Michael says. "There's friendship and kindness. We see each other often and have good feelings for one another."

Second son Christopher was "gregarious and a bit of a clown" as a child, according to his mother. He rarely showed his emotions, but when he did it was special. "In his funny, quiet way, a squeeze of the hand speaks volumes," Elizabeth said.

After graduating school, he met Aileen Getty, one of the fifteen grandchildren of the late oil tycoon John Paul Getty. Aileen was a mere nineteen years old, but she and Christopher fell deeply in love and wanted to marry. There was one hitch: if she married before turning twenty-two, she would lose her share of the $750 million Getty trust fund (about $500,000 a year).

"We've been desperately in love for a long time," she said. She begged and pleaded with the Getty trustees to get rid of the marriage condition, but that proved impossible. The three years seemed like a lifetime to the two young lovers.

After finally being allowed to marry in 1981, Christopher and Aileen started up an antique clothing boutique in Santa Barbara, California, but it failed because of a bad location in a residential area. They had two children, Caleb and Andrew, and moved up the California coast to Pebble Beach.

For a few years Christopher worked as a stained-glass artist and studied glassblowing. "He does beautiful work," says brother Michael.

Unfortunately, Christopher and Aileen's marriage soured in mid-1986. Despite all Elizabeth's pleas that they try to reconcile and work out their differences, Aileen filed for divorce in September of 1987.

As a little girl, Liza Todd was called "an independent tornado" by her mother. Elizabeth once said, "She looks so much like Mike—her mannerisms, the way she uses her hands, the way she shrugs her shoulders—and the larceny and con of her mind. It gives you the creeps. At one time the resemblance could make me run from the room crying. It was Mike. The only thing missing was a cigar."

While she was growing up, the adults around Liza admired her brains and flair. Once Richard Burton saw Peter O'Toole engaged in a deep discussion with the little girl. When Burton asked avowed-child-hater

O'Toole why, the actor answered, "Look, I'm no fool. I'm trying to get in good with her because in twenty years we're all going to have to go to her for jobs. She'll own the industry."

Despite her obvious brains and beauty (or maybe because of them), working in the entertainment industry is currently the furthest thing from Liza's mind. She completely shuns the public life and has followed her half-brother's steps into the artistic world. She bought a small farm in a tiny town in the Catskill Mountains in upstate New York where she sculpts horses which are exhibited in New York City galleries.

In 1984 Liza married another sculptor, Hap Tivey, in a small, private ceremony held at the home of some friends in upstate New York. Among the folksy entertainment was a country band and square dancing. The irony of her daughter's quiet wedding wasn't lost on Elizabeth, who commented that if Mike Todd had been alive, Liza would have had to get married in Madison Square Garden and wear a dress with a train stretching halfway across the building.

Liza had wanted to invite stepdad Burton to her nuptials, but Elizabeth wouldn't allow it. Seeing her ex was simply too painful. Sadly, the occasion would have been the young woman's last chance to see the great actor who was her stepfather—Richard Burton died a week later.

When Liza and Tivey had a son a year and a half later, they decided to let their child grow up with his own identity. Instead of naming him for any of his famous relatives, the boy was called Quinn C. A very low-key Liza casually lugs him around in a backpack.

Shy, "ugly duckling" Maria never felt like an

adopted child when growing up. Once she was squirming around on Elizabeth's bed when the star was trying to sleep. "Stop flapping your fins," her mother said. "You're exactly like your father." She was always treated exactly the same as the other three children.

Elizabeth was always afraid that Maria's shyness would prevent her from finding a boyfriend, and she would parade a long line of suitable suitors in front of her youngest daughter. As it turned out, she didn't need any help. Maria soon blossomed into a vivacious, beautiful woman and became a fashion model.

One night at the New York disco Studio 54, she was introduced to Steve Carson, the son of wealthy Florida orange growers. She says she looked "sort of tacky," and he says she looked "gorgeous." When he proposed, she put on her shoes backwards and felt "so dizzy and up in the clouds that I got lost round the city all day."

When they married on February 13, 1982, the wedding was splendid, but the rehearsal wasn't as quiet as they would have liked. As the "Wedding March" played in the background, Maria came down the stairway of a posh New York restaurant. Suddenly, loud rock music came blasting out of nowhere. A clock radio Elizabeth had brought had turned itself on, but no one could figure out how to turn it off. Finally Princess Grace (of Monaco) crawled under the table on her hands and knees and pulled the plug.

Maria was terribly excited when she discovered she was pregnant. "It's almost impossible to describe the anticipation—the specialness—I feel about having a child of my own flesh and blood," she told a journalist at the time. "My marriage will be long-lasting. The fact that there have been divorces in my parents' pasts doesn't scare me. I'm a separate person."

But Maria's marriage was far from perfect, despite her hopes and dreams. Maria ran up large phone bills seeking marital advice from her seven-times-married mother.

"Maria wants a more glamorous life, more like her mother's," Carson said at the time. "I'm not offering that. I want a family life-style. I'm devastated over the split. I'm still in shock."

Breaking up was terribly hard on Maria, as well, and she dreaded getting into a big custody battle with Carson over their daughter.

Although her mother had first advised Maria to make a clean break, Elizabeth later tried to get the couple back together. She recounted all her own divorces and said it's too easy to just break up in the heat of anger instead of sticking things out and trying to find solutions to problems. Then Elizabeth threw in the clincher—the fact that little Elizabeth would suffer terribly from the divorce.

Maria couldn't help remembering the pain she'd gone through when her mother and Richard Burton divorced, remarried, and then redivorced. She had loved both of her parents with all her heart and was shattered when they broke up. Deciding she'd been immature and overly hasty in leaving Carson, Maria went back home to begin her marriage anew.

Elizabeth's stepdaughter Kate Burton fondly remembers the summers she spent with her dad and Elizabeth on the sets of *Virginia Woolf* and *The Taming of the Shrew*. She still dreams of their fabulous cruises on the Mediterranean and Adriatic seas on the huge yacht *Kalizma.*

"Elizabeth and I got along well," says Kate, now an up-and-coming actress in her own right. "This is where everybody always says, 'Oh sure, really'—because I wasn't her child. So she didn't have to discipline me; she could have all the fun parts of me, she could enjoy me."

Another young actress looks at the experience of having Elizabeth for a stepmother a little differently. Says Carrie Fisher, daughter of Eddie Fisher and Debbie Reynolds, "I've always said that if I wasn't Debbie Reynolds' daughter, I'd make fun of whoever was," in reference to the famous furor caused by her dad's infatuation with Elizabeth.

She remembers well how painful it was when her father deserted her family for a new—albeit brief—life with Elizabeth. Although she has publicly criticized her father's actions, she's since forgiven him and made peace.

Elizabeth's children harbor no grudges against their mother. All of the star's children are "nice kids," according to Broadway columnist Radie Harris. "Elizabeth is a very good mother, and they have a very healthy relationship with her."

The star explains her relation with her children simply. "I never want to be one of those mothers who refuses to cut the umbilical cord," Elizabeth says. "If they want to go away, I'm not going to be a martyr. That would kill the relationship.

"My heart, my arms, my mind will always be open to my children. Though I would do anything at all for them, it is they who must live their own lives."

Her sensible attitude seems to have worked wonders. Some children of celebrities often cash in on their parents' fame and do everything they can to get their own names in the papers. Others have rejected their famous parents completely in their attempts to live separate lives. Sadly, more than a few have been so overcome by life and the burdens of fame that they turned to drugs or even suicide as a means of escaping.

Elizabeth's children have turned out exceedingly "normal," considering the sometimes circus-like circumstances they grew up in. They've taken care of their mother in her many times of trouble and were responsible for seeing that she entered the Betty Ford Center to fight her addictions. They were all present to celebrate her many extraordinary successes.

"I think Mom did a big job giving us as much peace and privacy as possible, considering her situation as a celebrity," Michael says.

As Maria says about her parents: "She makes me feel that I too can be and do anything I want. After all, it was they who taught us how precious love is."

# Chapter Eleven

*"Never has a disease left so many helpless—
leaving loved ones and families reaching out
only to frustration and fear."*
—Elizabeth Taylor

ONE would have thought that by early 1985 Elizabeth had more than enough to keep her occupied. She was dating a number of fascinating men, busily acting in television projects, keeping up with the joys and tribulations of her growing family, and still fighting the discomfort caused by her bad back.

Yet, there was a terrible affliction she kept reading about in the papers, seeing on TV, and hearing about in whispers from acquaintances all over the world. Hundreds of people were dying, thousands more infected; word of the Acquired Immune Deficiency Syndrome (AIDS) was on everyone's lips.

Everyone in the entertainment world knew of at least one colleague—if not a true friend—who had come down with the killer disease. The fear of catching the incurable illness played havoc with the minds of freewheeling, anything-goes seekers of easy good times.

Suddenly, every sexually active person from remote tropical islands to big-city high-rises was forced to consider the dire consequences that could arise from a one-night stand.

"The mores of today's society—the singles bars, the easy pickup—it's all going to have to change, and we're going to have to grow up," Elizabeth says.

Elizabeth saw the horror the disease was causing all over Hollywood and was deeply affected by the senseless deaths and agonizing pain all around her. Lacking a way to help find a cure, she began speaking to people about raising money for research into the dread disease. With great shock and disappointment, she found that many supposedly liberal and informed people would back off quickly, while giving her horrified looks, at the mere mention of the word *AIDS*.

"I won't tell you the names of some of the people [in Hollywood] who refused to have their names identified [with AIDS fund-raising], because it would blow your mind," she says.

She got mad—then she got to work. "It so angered me that I finally thought to myself, 'Bitch, do something yourself instead of sitting there just getting angry!'

"It had such an unbelievable stigma. . . .There was such a void, such a silence. So I just started opening my mouth.

"It was seven months later that I found out my friend Rock Hudson had AIDS. . . .But I was already committed."

When Elizabeth's longtime friend and *Giant* co-star came forward with the public announcement that he had AIDS in July 1985, it was thirteen months after the disease had been diagnosed and a mere ten weeks before his death.

Hudson's admission of having AIDS was probably the hardest thing he had to do in his life. Respected around the world as the rugged, handsome star of sixty-five movies and several TV series, Hudson usually played a squeaky-clean, wholesome, and very heterosexual leading man. He'd been married briefly to his agent's secretary, Phyllis Gates, after a fan magazine threatened to expose his inconspicuous homosexuality.

Elizabeth was never bothered one way or another by a friend's sexual preference. She'd known for years and years that close friends Monty Clift and Hudson were gay, but that never stopped her from socializing with them, spending vacations in their homes, or loving them deeply.

Her relationship with Hudson was such that she stayed in his Central Park West apartment during her run in *The Little Foxes*. Never known for being a tidy soul, Elizabeth messed up the place so badly that Hudson and his friend Tom Clark moved into a hotel until the play closed down. According to a friend of Hudson's, "The bathroom had makeup everywhere. Her dresses were everywhere. She'd get up in the middle of the night to eat and leave cheese on the couch. But Rock's attitude was, 'Let her make the apartment a mess. I love her like a sister—I'll go stay somewhere else.'"

AIDS had been big news before Hudson collapsed in Paris on July 21 after his treatments with the experimental drug HPA-23 had failed. After he admitted to having AIDS, however, reports about the disease seemed to eclipse everything else.

Nearly every major magazine and newspaper in the U.S. ran a cover story about the disease. Many people wanted to pass a law requiring mandatory blood tests before love scenes were shot. Wild rumors swept the entertainment industry about *this* big movie star having AIDS, or *that* famous ballet dancer, or *that* big singer who played in Vegas. Some felt that the AIDS scare was witch-hunting, eighties-style.

"This is a gossip community," said society columnist George Christy. "If someone loses five pounds, they suddenly become a candidate for AIDS."

The rumors about those afflicted with AIDS were almost never substantiated. The poor souls who lay gravely ill or had already died from the various illnesses which attack the body after it contracts AIDS were not public figures.

However, one would read notices—daily, it seemed —in the trade papers about a tragically young choreographer dying from leukemia, or a costume designer who died from pneumonia, or a director who died from meningitis. Gay people lived in fear that they would lose their jobs simply because of their sexual preference.

When Hudson came down with AIDS, the fingers immediately began wagging—he's gay, he's gay. At that time most people thought AIDS was a disease contracted only by "bad" people—such as homosexuals or intravenous drug users.

The wagging fingers disgusted Elizabeth because

she knew better. "It's going to take a famous heterosexual woman dying before it [AIDS] really gets the
attention of the heterosexual community," she said.

"People need so desperately to be educated. People
have to come to terms with the fact that it's a heterosexual disease. We're having a hard time doing that."

She also knew that just because someone gets AIDS,
it doesn't mean that that person is one of the dregs of
society. Elizabeth herself has many close homosexual
friends who are upstanding citizens, and her fourth
husband—the crooner, idol of millions—publicly admitted his own drug use by injection just a few years
ago.

Elizabeth went about setting the record straight—
and raising funds for a cure—with a vengeance. She
didn't give a hoot how unpopular a cause it was. If
anything, that only made the idea more attractive to
her. As a converted Jew, she's had to put up with some
of the intolerance and prejudice which has plagued
members of that religion, and she saw how being a
member of a minority affected three of her husbands:
Todd and Fisher (both Jewish), and Burton (Welsh).

"Because Elizabeth has been through so much tragedy herself, she can easily understand the agony of
others," said one Hollywood source. "She's always
ready to help a friend, no matter what the trouble or
problem is.

"All that pain and tragedy she's suffered has made
her terribly attractive to gay men. For some reason
they adore women who have suffered and lived life to
its fullest. Gay men put women like Liz, Marilyn
Monroe, and Judy Garland on a pedestal."

Appalled by the nation's ignorance about AIDS as well as by the devastation wrought by the disease, Elizabeth immediately began planning a big benefit dinner for the AIDS Project of Los Angeles. Once her glittery name landed in the ring, dozens of stars emerged to lend a hand.

In the midst of planning the September 19 "Commitment to Life" dinner, Hudson announced that he had AIDS. "I've handled a hundred dinners, and when the news started about Rock Hudson, I've never seen anything take off like this one," said Lucille Polachek of Events Unlimited, which sold the $250- and $500-a-person tickets.

"Rock's illness helped give AIDS a face," said actress Morgan Fairchild. "Sometimes people will listen more to celebrities than to a doctor somewhere in a newspaper."

Comedienne Joan Rivers couldn't agree more. "Two years ago when I hosted a benefit for AIDS, I couldn't get one major star to turn out," she said. "It ended up being just me and a transvestite onstage. I received death threats and hate mail. Rock's admission is a horrendous way to bring AIDS to the attention of the American public, but by doing so, Rock, in his life, has helped millions in the process."

Nearly three thousand people crowded into the ballroom of the Los Angeles Westin Bonaventure Hotel to see Betty Ford presented with the Commitment to Life award. Luminaries included Angie Dickinson, Whoopi Goldberg, Marsha Mason, Kate Jackson, George Hamilton, Phyllis Diller, Abigail van Buren, Richard Dreyfuss, Jane Seymour, and Gina Lollobrigida.

The entertainment was spectacular: Cyndi Lauper and Rod Stewart sang a duet; Sam Harris, Diahann Carroll, Sammy Davis Jr., and Carol Burnett sang an homage to Broadway; and comic Steven Wright told jokes. Between acts, Mayor Tom Bradley, Shirley MacLaine, Phil Donahue, and Marlo Thomas all spoke, and asked for pledges.

Burt Reynolds read a telegram from President Reagan. Burt Lancaster read some stirring words from Hudson, who was too ill to attend. "I'm not happy that I have AIDS, but . . . I have been told that the media coverage of my own situation has brought enormous international attention to the gravity of this disease . . . and is leading to more research, more contribution of funds, a better understanding of AIDS than ever before."

Elizabeth, the evening's hostess, declared, "Tonight is the start of my personal war on this disease, AIDS."

The evening brought in more than one million dollars. Hudson himself donated $250,000 to the cause.

Weeks later it was revealed that Hudson hadn't actually penned the speech Lancaster had delivered. At that time the famed actor weighed only ninety-seven pounds and was nearly comatose.

"The statement wasn't written by Rock," admitted the actor's longtime friend and former manager Tom Clark. "But can't we just say they were his thoughts? Those words have been so encouraging to so many millions. Let him have those words as his legacy."

Others, such as producer Ross Hunter, said that Hudson never even knew he had the dread disease; that his name was being used to solicit funds without his consent. "Every time I try to tell the truth, people have misquoted me," Hunter said after Hudson's death. "My friend is at peace, and that's the way I'd like to leave it. I can't get it out of my mind. It's been like a ghost following me. Can you imagine what would happen if I said anything that was against what Elizabeth said, or any of the others?"

A week after the benefit, Elizabeth held a press conference to announce that she would head a national group, uniting the local AIDS fund-raising organizations in L.A. and New York. Her black hair lightly streaked with silver was brushed back from her face on the sides, with bangs in front and spikes on top. Putting on her glasses, she said that the new organization was called the American Foundation for AIDS Research (AmFAR).

"We plan to muster the talent and energy of America's brightest scientific and medical researchers to solve the mysteries of AIDS. We are prepared to do what it takes to find a cure," she said.

During this time she frequently visited her pal Hudson as he lay wasting away, first in his bed at the UCLA Medical Center, and later at his home. She also sent a phalanx of security guards to keep the reporters and weeping fans at bay.

After Hudson's death on October 2, a grieving Elizabeth took it upon herself to arrange a memorial service for her friend. Although born a Catholic, Hudson had never been a regular churchgoer, and holding a religious service would have been hypocritical. Instead, Elizabeth helped to arrange a joyous, upbeat event which would do justice to the actor's love of parties and good times.

"The music played at my funeral will be played in boogie," Hudson had told his close friend Jim Matteoni as a teenager.

Elizabeth sent out telegrams to Hudson's relatives and closest friends, and about 150 of them showed up at his huge Beverly Hills home on the evening of October 19. The guests were checked over by security guards several times on their way up the long walkway to the house, and at the door they were greeted by Elizabeth and Tom Clark.

After sitting down on the folding chairs placed under a canopy in Hudson's garden overlooking the sunset and the San Fernando Valley, Father Terry Sweeney began the service with a short eulogy describing the actor's great talents and courage.

Elizabeth got up next and recalled some of the precious times she'd spent in Hudson's company. Her laughter mingled with her tears as she recalled the night the two of them invented what they thought was a marvelous new drink—a chocolate margarita.

Carol Burnett told the group the funny incidents which occurred when she toured with Hudson in *I Do! I Do!;* then John Schuck (one of Hudson's co-stars on *McMillan and Wife*) and actress Constance Towers sang two of the deceased's favorite songs from the play: "My Cup Runneth Over" and "Roll up the Ribbons." After a few more brief speeches, the guests were invited up to a terrace to listen to a mariachi band, drink margaritas, and indulge in a lavish buffet.

Meanwhile, helicopters with photographers hanging out the doors were circling overhead and Hudson's next-door neighbor was selling wake-view seats on her property for $300 each.

After Elizabeth got a grip on her grief and the hubbub surrounding Hudson's death began to die down, she and actress Audrey Hepburn went to an AIDS fund-raiser in Paris.

Undaunted by reported threats on her life, the beautiful star continued to do whatever she could to aid victims of the ravaging disease. Patients awaiting death at San Francisco General Hospital's Ward 5-A like to chat in a room they call the Elizabeth Taylor room because the wall is dominated by a huge poster of the actress dressed in slinky black lingerie.

When a patient was asked why Elizabeth's poster graces the wall of a ward filled mostly with gay male patients, he answered, "Because it's fun and there's life in it." The room is named after her "because she was not afraid to come here and visit us; she had the guts to show that AIDS is not spread casually and that we are not lepers."

In May 1986, Elizabeth's appearance before the Senate Appropriations Labor and Health Subcommittee made the front pages. In front of her ex-husband John Warner, she pleaded with the subcommittee to increase the stipend of governmental money used to fund AIDS research work.

"Since my friend Rock Hudson died of AIDS last year . . . I have become familiar with the tragedy of AIDS and I am acutely aware of research funding needs," she said.

"A comprehensive, sustained basic research effort

will pay off in many ways. It will greatly increase our ability to understand, prevent, and treat not only cancer and AIDS but many other intractable chronic diseases such as arthritis and multiple sclerosis, which—like AIDS—involve virus-induced malfunction of the immune system."

After wooing the Senate, Elizabeth went back to more traditional fund-raising methods. Arriving only an hour late on the arm of fashion designer Calvin Klein, Elizabeth next hosted an AIDS benefit for the fashion industry, which brought in $500,000.

Two days after the event, a star-struck Klein was still talking about his date with Elizabeth. "She kept me waiting two hours, and it was wonderful!" he gushed.

In June she convinced friends Carole Bayer Sager and Burt Bacharach to donate all the proceeds from their song "That's What Friends Are For" to AmFAR. The song, recorded by Dionne Warwick, Elton John, Stevie Wonder, and Gladys Knight was expected to bring in at least $600,000. To thank the songwriters, she hosted a spectacular $1,000-a-ticket dinner at the Kirkeby Mansion (home of the old TV series *The Beverly Hillbillies*).

The second "Commitment to Life" benefit in September brought in close to $1 million, and Elizabeth was honored with the award. The following June, Elizabeth was able to raise $2.5 million at a fund-raiser in Washington. (Checks for $1 million were given by both Malcolm Forbes and an eighty-eight-year-old Japanese philanthropist, Ryoichi Sasakawa, whom Elizabeth had met during a recent trip to Japan.)

Thanks to the hard work of volunteers such as Elizabeth, the donations continue to pour in, but the disease is still spreading in epidemic proportion and no cure has been found. Debates over mandatory AIDS testing and isolation for patients also rage unabated.

But if Elizabeth has her way, the cure will be found as soon as possible. "Each of us has a responsibility to do our part in defeating this tragic epidemic," she says. "I pray that you will join me in waging this war so that we may soon see the day when AIDS will be but a painful memory. We will win—we *must* win—for the sake of all humanity."

# Chapter Twelve

*"It's best not to underestimate Elizabeth. No one has been 'finished, washed up' more times than she has. And yet she always comes back stronger than ever."—Zef Bufman*

CONFIDENT that she was doing everything possible to raise funds for AIDS, Elizabeth decided that it was high time to stretch her artistic muscles a little. When her longtime pal Robert Wagner asked her to co-star with him in a TV movie, she batted her double rows of eyelashes, smiled her prettiest, and said yes.

*There Must Be a Pony* was produced by Wagner's own R. J. Productions. He needed the star power of Elizabeth's name to obtain the $3.2 million necessary to make the film, and she needed him to make sure the picture kept its integrity.

Although it marked the first time they had acted together, Elizabeth and Wagner have known each other since they were children eating sandwiches and drinking lemonade during pool parties at Roddy McDowall's house. She was already a big star by the time he made his first movie in 1950, and they grew closer as the years—and various marriages—went on.

Of Natalie Wood, Elizabeth says, "Nat and I were great friends. The four of us would spend weekends together. It was R.J. and Natalie and the gentleman I was married to at the time," Elizabeth sniffs, rather than mentioning Eddie Fisher's name.

After the Wagners divorced because Natalie fell in love with her *Splendor in the Grass* co-star Warren Beatty, Wagner went to Rome and visited Elizabeth on the *Cleopatra* set. "The electricity that this one generated . . ." he says, pointing to her. "She would walk into some damned club in Rome and people would go crazy."

Both stars adamantly deny that they have ever been lovers, but their friendship is definitely a special one. "I have been with Elizabeth through the high points and low points, and she has been with me," he comments.

After Natalie Wood—then remarried to Wagner— drowned, Elizabeth was the first one to arrive at the Wagner house, offering what comfort she could. "R.J. knows I'll always be there for him," she says fondly. "It's that simple."

The two old friends greatly enjoyed working together. Elizabeth played an actress who was placed in a mental hospital after suffering a serious breakdown and tries to revive her career with the help of her new love (Wagner) after she finally gets out.

One of their favorite parts of filming the movie was their first love scene together. Elizabeth said the communication between their eyes was complete, and Wagner laughed that it was worth the long time he'd had to wait for that magical moment.

The critics weren't quite so happy with the resulting film. *People* magazine suggested that viewers tape the program on their VCRs, then fast-forward through it, watching only Elizabeth's scenes. "Think of this as a one-woman show, Elizabeth Taylor's show, and you'll be in for some moments to remember." Reviewer Jeff Jarvis called the script "thin" and says "the plot makes as much sense as most of the people in that [mental] ward would."

Never one to let mediocre reviews bother her, Elizabeth was already off on the arm of a handsome new escort—George Hamilton—picking up one of the most esteemed awards in cinedom. Elizabeth was so "thrilled" to be honored with the Film Society of Lincoln Center's prestigious tribute to "a significant film artist" that she brought two new dresses into her peony-filled $1,800-a-night suite at the Plaza Athénée so she could pick out the one she wanted to wear at the last minute.

Deciding must have been hard, because Elizabeth was supposed to walk onstage forty-five minutes before she showed up wearing a dazzling Arnold Scaasi gown of gray, black, and silver organza petals, showing off shoulders that could have belonged to a teenager.

An audience of 2,700 gave her a five-minute standing ovation, then watched Elizabeth virtually cringe as clips from her long movie career were shown. "I hope you're not bored. I hate seeing myself on the screen, I'm so dying," she explained.

"I was thrilled when I first heard of plans for this evening, then I heard who my predecessors were [Charlie Chaplin, Laurence Olivier, Barbara Stanwyck, Alfred Hitchcock, Bob Hope, John Huston, and Federico Fellini]. I thought I had better send them a retrospective of my reviews. They must have made a mistake!

"But after watching all the incredible hard work that went into tonight, I guess they really did mean me. I feel very special and cared for."

Before leaving the stage Elizabeth paid a grand tribute to her eighty-nine-year-old mother, Sara. "There's just one person I'd like to thank, first for giving me birth, and for being there for me all of my life—my mother," the actress said.

Now that Elizabeth was steadily appearing on the tanned arm of George Hamilton, the gossip magazines began to print screaming headlines that he was about to become husband number seven. The two were frequently seen at the trendiest night spots and star-studded parties around the world: Spago in Hollywood, Aspinall's in London (where they spent $3,000 a night for adjoining rooms), Arab billionaire Adnan Khashoggi's estate in Spain.

They both reveled in the good times they had together. Sometimes when they went out to dinner, Hamilton would send the waiter out to buy a hundred dollars' or two hundred dollars' worth of lottery tickets; and they would sit delightedly rubbing off the silver coating like children on Christmas. Once he even hired a Boeing 727 and took the lovely lady and some pals to a posh dinner up in the clouds.

Of course, they did have their spats. Hamilton bought her a $5,000 pendant which spelled out "Liz" in diamonds. She was so angry—hating the nickname ever since her brother Howard would call her "Lizzy the Cow" or "Liz the Lizard" when they were kids—that she had Hamilton send the necklace back and have the remaining letters in her proper name added, at a cost of many thousands of dollars. Another time when she took him to dinner at Spago, he wandered off and was quickly surrounded by lovely young women. Elizabeth was overheard saying, "Tell Mr. Hamilton to get his suntanned keister over here right now or find his own way home." Her forty-eight-year-old escort was back at her side in a flash.

Friends thought they made a perfect couple. "George keeps her on her toes," said one pal. "He's a looks-and-health fanatic. He won't let her slip. He looks fantastic; as long as she's with him, she has to keep up."

Elizabeth and Hamilton both laughed at all the gossip they were creating and continually denied any impending wedding bells.

"No matter what you say and how many times you say it," Elizabeth said, "they're not going to believe it. Otherwise they wouldn't keep asking."

"But they'll eventually find out. One year from now. Two years from now. Ten years from now. When we're still not married, maybe they'll believe us."

Occasionally one or the other would even be seen with a different date (he with actress Allene Simmons and ex-wife Alana; she with singer Bob Dylan and international financier Sir Gordon White) but the rumors and marriage-date speculations continued to fly unabated, especially after they spent Christmas 1986, together in Gstaad. She returned in a wheelchair after hurting her knee "playing hide'n'seek with George."

Elizabeth included Hamilton in her next TV movie —*Poker Alice.* She enjoyed making her first Western in more than sixty movies and played a no-nonsense gambling lady who wins a whorehouse during a poker game on a train. Hamilton played her puppy-dog-faithful cousin who made no bones about his infatuation with the beautiful cardplayer.

Press materials describe Alice as a "red-blooded lady who likes red-blooded men," which made Elizabeth giggle, "My kind of a lady."

Hamilton calls Elizabeth "a child, wonderfully naive," and director Arthur Allen Seidelman sees her as "a little girl but don't be misled. This lady is no push-over."

Although Seidelman was told by Elizabeth's long-time publicist Chen Sam that he would have to establish himself as the boss early or she would "walk all over" him, the actress still got all her star perks. One hundred thousand dollars of the film's budget was allocated to giving her presents.

Each and every day during the twenty-two-day shoot, another expensive bauble was handed over in a different, imaginative manner. One was delivered by Pony Express. Another arrived on a stagecoach. A magician pulled one out from behind her ear. The bank on the set was robbed, and her gift was found in the vault. A male chorus sang "Liz" (to the tune of "Mame") and kick-stepped over with her present. Each gift averaged $4,500. Included were: a jeweled stickpin from Cartier, a Van Cleef and Arpels travel clock, an engraved gold whistle, necklaces and matching earrings, and a handmade Indian silver belt.

"Oooo," she squealed, slipping on a gold and lapis necklace. "It's fabulous!" Each offering brought a delighted smile to her ruby lips.

During the filming of *Alice* in Tucson, Arizona, Elizabeth turned fifty-five. The producers sent out invitations with a picture from *Lassie Come Home* and a caption reading: "Guess who's having a birthday—and it isn't Lassie." The seventy-member Phoenix Boys Choir sang "Happy Birthday," and her gifts included a leather director's chair with matching footstool.

Then Hamilton arrived with his own little offering—wrapped up in a huge box. "I want to give you a horse blanket, a little something made of squirrel," he said.

Elizabeth hungrily clawed off the paper and shook out a $50,000 mink walking jacket with a front zipper, wide collar, and pleated cuffs. Trying it on, she said, "Oh my God, I cannot believe it. It's so soft, it feels like sable."

"No, darling," he replied after receiving his kiss. "It's moon-dust mink."

"It's not from around here. You got it in New York?"

"No, it's not from around here. I had to search all over for this. It's hard to get rat up here in the mountains," Hamilton joked.

The next day Elizabeth and Hamilton flew back to Los Angeles to attend a party at the home of Burt Bacharach and Carole Bayer Sager. Looking radiant in a low-cut white dress and loads of diamonds, Elizabeth arrived just in time to try her chocolate cake—an hour and a half late. The guests included Shirley Maclaine, Barry Manilow, Bette Midler, Whoopi Goldberg, Michael Jackson, Bette Davis, Joan Collins, Charles Bronson, and Jill Ireland. Stevie Wonder, Dionne Warwick, and Melissa Manchester all serenaded the birthday girl.

Back on the set in Tucson the next day, the crew continued to pamper their star. Dressing a woman in period costumes with corsets, hats, and elaborate hair-styles is no easy feat—especially when the star is Elizabeth Taylor, who needs to have each exacting detail just right.

"They treat her as if she's Queen Elizabeth—not Elizabeth Taylor," said one stagehand.

The royal treatment was reflected on the screen when the film aired in May 1987, as well. Elizabeth looked simply gorgeous in *Poker Alice.* Her Nolan Miller costumes were stunning and fit her slim new figure perfectly. Unfortunately, the film's script was dull and the acting insipid—but Elizabeth's looks were to die for.

Howard Rosenberg of the Los Angeles *Times* said, "The biggest question these days is not how Taylor performs on the screen, but how she looks. Well, she looks great. Otherwise this is a flat, overlit, pedestrian, humdrum, drag-along movie that wastes not only Taylor . . . but also Tom Skerritt [her bounty-hunter love interest]."

*USA Today*'s Monica Collins said, "Watching Liz Taylor in a TV movie is like watching a dinosaur in a party dress dance down the street. You stand back and gawk."

After collecting her $1 million fee for *Poker Alice,* Elizabeth went home to relax for a while. Her three-story mansion is tucked in among pine trees and California cypresses in the hills of Bel Air, and is surrounded by an elaborate security system of stone walls, fences, and wrought-iron grillwork. She purchased it from Frank Sinatra's ex-wife Nancy for two million dollars soon after separating from John

Warner, and immediately added on a new wing. It is now worth an estimated five million dollars.

The monochrome, off-white living room has honey-colored parquet floors, a thick Aubusson carpet, and eighteenth-century English furniture. Here and there are puffy cushions and needlework-covered foot-stools. A table is covered with silver-framed photos of Elizabeth with her famous friends and lovers. The only colors come from the huge arrangements of orchids and other exotic flowers and the millions of dollars of art lining the walls: a Renoir, a Degas, a Monet, a Modigliani, a Van Gogh, and a few Utrillos thrown in for good luck.

The house has several guest rooms on the first and third floors, a library, and a TV/projection room. The entire second floor is made up of Elizabeth's private rooms—a sitting room, bedroom, bath, and dressing rooms. Even the bathrooms are filled with the cloying scent of exotic flowers and decorated with rare works of art.

For once, her menagerie of pets have been house-trained, and her chaos is kept orderly by housekeeper/secretary/Cordon Bleu chef—Elizabeth Thorburn.

Elizabeth's normal day begins at 9:00 A.M. when she breakfasts in bed then smokes a cigarette. Thorburn reads off the day's appointments, which Elizabeth decides to attend or cancel depending on her mood.

After rising, she may decide to go shopping. In that case she merely walks downstairs to her living room, for every store in town sends her sample styles to try on. Even Tiffany delivers to her. Once she decides to get dressed, it's a major operation, sometimes taking up to two and a half hours to get her hair, makeup, and outfit just right.

Every day that the star is in residence, she insists on having an English-style tea served promptly at 4:00 P.M. Other meals are never at set times—she may have lunch in Beverly Hills with a gal pal, suddenly decide to eat supper at a hot new restaurant in New York, or invite ten people in for a sit-down dinner party.

She gets bored easily, which accounts for her energy and constant stream of new projects. "I'm loud, noisy, earthy, and ready for much more living," Elizabeth says with a smile.

Elizabeth's zest for life was clearly shown by the way she jumped into the creation and promotion of her first retail product—the perfume Elizabeth Taylor's Passion.

She chose the name because it is the one word which best reflects her life and the way she lives it. "I have a passion for love, food, children, and animals," she says. "I have a passion for life in everything I do."

For years she has purchased four or five different perfumes and worn them in layers to create the floral/ Oriental scent she desired. When Parfums International approached her about finding just the right blend she's been searching for, she jumped at the chance.

"I was involved all the way with choosing the scent," she says. Various mixtures were brought to her labeled only with numbers—no hint to what they contained. "I had to go by my nose."

When the scent was introduced at the Robinson's department store in Beverly Hills on September 14, 1987, a crowd of over two thousand people waited hours in sweltering heat to glimpse the star. She was characteristically forty-five minutes late, and people were beginning to hiss and boo as the never-ending Passion promo video began showing once again on the twelve color TV screens flanking the purple-draped stage set up between the china and linen departments.

"I promise that Miss Taylor is on her way," said a store spokeswoman in answer to the public's cries of "We want Liz!" Restless fans began stealing the large posters featuring the star and a bottle of her purple perfume.

When she at long last arrived, her aura swept the crowd up. Everyone began smiling and clapping as the bright TV lights turned on and hundreds of camera strobes lit the area with bursts of electronic lightning.

She looked absolutely gorgeous in a purple Nolan Miller dress, with long sleeves, a surplice closing and hem just above her knees. One fan, having trouble seeing her slight five-foot, four-inch frame above the crush of people, asked her to stand up on a chair, and she laughed that such a move would surely lead to disaster.

"I was so nervous about coming," she said. "This is the first time I've made a public appearance like this. I want to talk to you—please feel free to ask me questions."

The crowd pressed forward, eager to speak to the superstar and hear her replies. She answered the wide range of questions—from retirement plans ("I never think about it") to how long a woman's passion can last ("as long as she lives")—with poise and charming wit. She graciously thanked fans who came from as far as Phoenix, Arizona, and told one man who said he'd seen her in both of her plays that he must be "very brave," and that she's "far too lazy to ever perform on Broadway again."

One woman presented her with a stuffed rabbit sporting a purple ribbon around its neck because Passion wasn't tested on animals. "Let me have my bunny," the star cried, reaching out, then hugged the toy to her.

Elizabeth will get a royalty from each $165-an-ounce bottle of Passion, and a percentage of the money will go to AIDS research.

Probably a good portion of the extra Passion spending money will be spent on more glamorous sparklers, such as the late Duchess of Windsor's $623,000 1935-era plume and crown diamond clip Elizabeth purchased after making a phone call from her poolside to the auction in Geneva.

"It is the first important jewel I have ever bought for myself," she admitted. "I felt so guilty, it seems so indulgent. I've never spent that much on myself before."

Elizabeth showed off her glamorous new pin on the bodice of her low-cut black and white halter dress while playing hostess during the flamboyant seventieth-anniversary party of billionaire Malcolm Forbes' financial magazine *Forbes*. Although Hamilton was also present, Elizabeth greeted guests at the side of her longtime friend Forbes and was seen holding his hand and kissing him during the evening. He gave her a check for one million dollars for AIDS research, and she called him her "million-dollar baby."

"What I do, I do to enjoy life and to promote my

business," Forbes said. "The million-dollar contribution to the campaign against AIDS was given to give *Forbes* Magazine's celebration more significance."

One of the richest men in America, Forbes owns a seventy-five-acre estate in New Jersey, a chateau in France, a ranch in Colorado, a palace in Tangier, and a 150-foot yacht called *The Highlander* that has fourteen bathrooms with gold fixtures, five staterooms, six salons, a wine cellar, and a sauna. His collection of priceless Fabergé eggs is among the most extensive in the world.

At the party he had a hundred bagpipers march over hills toward a thirteen-by-twenty-foot replica of a Scottish castle, where the floodlights reflected off the artificial fog he had pumped in. The 1,100 guests dined on a lavish feast served by 302 waiters, danced in a circus-sized tent, and watched a show combining the music of Gershwin and Beethoven with a spectacular display of fireworks. One guest said it was the first time he'd ever seen limo gridlock on the ground as twenty-three helicopters fought for airspace overhead.

Of course their liaison—which included Forbes giving Elizabeth a fifty-mile ride around his property on one of his many Harley-Davidson motorcycles (and later on, a purple Harley for her very own), and dinners at the 21 Club and Le Cirque—immediately provided more grist for the rumor mills. One friend predicted a long, happy friendship "because Malcolm is one of the few remaining bachelors in the world who can really afford her. She can never resist dashing, rich men—especially if they're single."

Nor can "dashing, rich men" resist her, *especially* if they're single.

Looking at her now, it's nearly impossible to believe that this svelte lady dressed in glamorous, tight-fitting gowns and adorned with dazzling gems is the same 175-pound blimp who appeared on the cover of *Hollywood Babylon II.* Plastic surgeons looking at her photos say that she's had at least two face-lifts—one soon after leaving the Betty Ford Center to tuck up the fifty pounds she lost, and the other a couple of years later.

One source swears that her Beverly Hills knife wielder gave her a face-lift, chemical peel, and tummy tuck for more than $10,000 during late 1986.

Syndicated columnist Erma Bombeck once complained that the hands are the only reliable way to tell a person's age nowadays. "They're a bas-relief map of life, so to speak," she wrote. "It's probably the only part of Elizabeth Taylor left over from *National Velvet.*"

Regardless of who did what to Elizabeth—or how much it cost—the spectacular results were well worth all the pain and expense.

After finishing her Passion promotion tour, Elizabeth plans to fly off to Italy and Brazil to film *The Young Toscanini,* directed by Franco Zeffirelli. It will be her first feature film since *The Mirror Crack'd* in 1980.

"It's a wonderful role, almost written for her," Zeffirelli said. "This role is almost like a cheerful Maria Callas, a great diva. And the last diva is Elizabeth Taylor today. I think we're going to watch [her] great comeback."

Elizabeth was studying operatic music and lip-synching for her role as Nadina Bulischoff, a Russian soprano who reigned supreme at Italy's La Scala opera house. When she toured Brazil, the last emperor of that land fell in love with her and she retired to be by his side. Three years later, an eighteen-year-old cellist —Toscanini—wanted Bulischoff to make a comeback in *Aida.* She believed the young man was just a delivery boy, but he convinced her that his age was relative— and gave her the confidence she needed to return to the stage. In the end, he conducts her.

The movie will be filled with music—both opera and jazz. "It's very funny, too," Zeffirelli adds. "The kind of humor only Elizabeth Taylor can do."

Elizabeth is definitely an extraordinary, one-of-a-kind woman. Any other mere mortal would surely have succumbed to the vast variety of illnesses and stresses she's endured. At the rate she was going in the early 1980s, the combination of her weight plus her overindulgence in booze and dependency on sleeping pills could easily have killed her.

Yet she survived it all—with her mesmerizing looks, dreamy life-style, and vast talents completely intact, possibly even enhanced. Like a phoenix, she dove into the fire and came out completely renewed.

The new Elizabeth Taylor is an amazing, wondrous woman. She is truly back—better and more beautiful than ever before.

# HOLLYWOOD'S
# LEADING LADIES

**JULIE CHRISTIE** by Michael Feeney Callan
The first biography of the beautiful and enigmatic star. Includes 8 pages of photos.
_____ 90209-3   $3.50 U.S.   _____ 90210-7   $4.50 Can.

**AUDREY HEPBURN** by Ian Woodward
Fascinating details of this captivating actress are revealed for the first time ever. With 8 pages of enchanting photos.
_____ 90076-7   $3.50 U.S.

**MARY TYLER MOORE** by Jason Bonderoff
Behind the famous smile of America's sweetheart lies a life of heartbreak, struggle, failure, and ultimate triumph!
_____ 90413-4   $3.95 U.S.   _____ 90414-2   $4.95 Can.

**KIM NOVAK: RELUCTANT GODDESS**
by Peter Harry Brown
The stunning true story of her superstardom, with 16 pages of fascinating photos.
_____ 90495-9   $3.95 U.S.   _____ 90496-7   $4.95 Can.

**JULIE ANDREWS** by Robert Windeler
The high and low notes of Hollywood's sweetest voice, including 8 pages of photos.
_____ 90514-9   $3.95 U.S.   _____ 90525-4   $4.95 Can.

# THE BRIGHTEST STARS...

**MERYL STREEP: RELUCTANT SUPERSTAR by Diana Maychick**
The first biography of this dazzling, articulate film star. With 8 pages of photos.
_____ 90246-8   $3.50 U.S.          _____ 90248-4   $4.50 Can.

**ROBERT DE NIRO: THE HERO BEHIND THE MASKS by Keith McKay**
A revealing look at one of today's most brilliant actors. Includes 16 pages of photos.
_____ 90475-4   $3.95 U.S.          _____ 90476-2   $4.95 Can.

**ROBERT DUVALL: HOLLYWOOD MAVERICK by Judith Slawson**
Leading the new breed of Hollywood hero. With 8 pages of dramatic photos.
_____ 90422-3   $3.95 U.S.          _____ 90423-1   $4.95 Can.

**KATHLEEN TURNER by Rebecca Stefoff**
The first biography of Hollywood's newest, sexy—and very daring—superstar. With 8 pages of glorious photos.
_____ 90604-8   $3.50 U.S.          _____ 90605-6   $4.50 Can.


ST. MARTIN'S PRESS—MAIL SALES
175 Fifth Avenue, New York, NY 10010

Please send me the book(s) I have checked above. I am enclosing a check or money order (not cash) for $_____ plus 75¢ per order to cover postage and handling (New York residents add applicable sales tax).

Name _____

Address_____

City _____ State_____ Zip Code_____
Allow at least 4 to 6 weeks for delivery                    30

Allow at least 4 to 6 weeks for delivery